LIVING THE ETERNAL WAY

A Spiritual Training Course

LIVING THE ETERNAL WAY

Spiritual Meaning
and Practice for
Daily Life

Ellen Grace O'Brian

CENTER FOR SPIRITUAL ENLIGHTENMENT

Book design by Amy Sibiga
Editing by Judith Pynn and Anne Cawley
Cover design by Clarice Hirata, Hirata Design
Cover photograph from PhotoDisc®
Cover photograph of author by Gabrielle Antolovich
Text photographs by Michael Scott (pages 47, 77) Ellen Grace
    O'Brian (pages 27, 37, 147) and Weststock (pages 4, 16, 95)

ISBN Number: 0-9660518-0-7
Library of Congress Catalog Card Number: 97-75320

Center for Spiritual Enlightenment
World Headquarters
1146 University Avenue
San Jose, CA 95126
Voice (408) 283-0221
CSE@best.com
www.CSEcenter.org

DEDICATION

The holy fires said among themselves: "The students of the sacred way have practiced self-discipline and tended us well. Thus we will teach them." Then they said to the students: "Life is God, Joy is God, All is God."

— Adapted from the *Chandogya Upanishad*

To the holy fire of the divine Self burning in every heart. . .

ACKNOWLEDGEMENTS

I acknowledge with respect, appreciation, and reverence the great teachers of the Eternal Way, whose lives and teachings reveal Divine Presence and shine light upon the path for seeking souls.

I am profoundly grateful to those whose spiritual teaching and presence has touched my life—Paramahansa Yogananda and Roy Eugene Davis, to Sri Satya Sai Baba, and to Dr. Aminah Raheem for guidance and inspiration.

To Anne Cawley, whose vision, spiritual commitment, many hours of work, patience, and compassion made this book possible, I say thank you from the bottom of my heart. To the friend who believed in the possibility of this work and supported it, to all the students over the years who attended classes at the Center and worked with this material, to those students yet to come, blessings of the Eternal Way to you.

Part One: The Eternal Way

Part Two: Living the Way

Introduction

In response to the question, "How does the desire for eternal life arise?" the great sage Ramana Maharshi replied, "Because the present state is unbearable. Why? Because it is not your True Nature." Like many seekers on the spiritual path I was looking for a way to find peace in my life, an inner happiness that would be unshakable in the turbulence of modern life. My earliest memories include a sense of spiritual yearning, wanting to know the truth about life, about my own self, and about God. Raised without a formal religious training from my family but growing up in a multi-cultural neighborhood, I was exposed to many different religions and spiritual teachings. I came away from those experiences knowing that God dwells in every church, temple, and synagogue—that no one person or religion had exclusive ownership of the sacred. I also knew the sacred was accessible, that it could be experienced and known, and that this experience could be life changing. What I did not know was how to access this sense of the sacred in any predictable way, nor did I understand how my ideas about God were themselves a barrier to finding what I was looking for. I thought I was looking for Something outside of my own nature. Although I sensed the nearness of the Divine Presence I did not know where or how to search for It. I certainly had heard it taught that the sacred "kingdom/queendom" is within but I did not know how to "enter" the temple within. After years of spiritual searching I was introduced to the path of Kriya Yoga, the spiritual practice rooted in the ancient Vedic teachings of the Eternal Way. The philosophy and practice of yoga was the sacred key that provided access, allowing me to enter the holy temple within. This book is about that key and the entryway—the Eternal Way of awakening from the illusion of separateness to the recovery of our true nature as one with the divine Self.

The Eternal Way refers to the teachings arising from the Vedas, the sacred literature of India that bears witness to the revelations of illumined seers dating back thousands of years. The word Veda means "revealed truth." From the philosophical foundation of Vedic revelation arose the disciplines of yoga, a systematic approach to spiritual realization. While the Vedic teachings have their historical origins in India and comprise the core of the Hindu religion, the essence of the Vedas extends beyond the boundaries of religion. The practice of yoga is not in and of itself a religion, but an individual path of authentic spiritual realization. Through the practice of yoga, as one awakens to revealed truth, the inner way of their own particular religion becomes known. Christians can become better Christians, Buddhists better Buddhists as a result of their yoga practice.

Kriya Yoga is the branch of yoga discipline brought to the United States by the Indian saint Paramahansa Yogananda in the early part of this century. His teachings, and those of others including Ramakrishna's disciple Swami Vivekenanda, have taken root in this country and are now blossoming. I was blessed to be introduced to these sacred teachings by Roy Eugene Davis, a direct disciple of Yogananda.

I appreciate deeply the gift of the enlightenment teaching and the many men and women, who have dedicated their lives to bring forth its message of freedom. I thank the authors whose work make the teaching available today. The works of Roy Eugene Davis and S. Radhakrishnan provided inspiration for many of the passages from the *Bhagavad Gita* paraphrased in this book. For insight into Patanjali's *Yoga Sutra*, I found the commentaries of Roy Eugene Davis, Georg Feuerstein, and Barbara Stoller Miller especially helpful.

This book was written for students of the Eternal Way—for those who are seeking to travel the inner path of soul realization. The Kriya Yoga "map" of this inner way is based on the philosophical treatise outlined in Patanjali's *Yoga Sutra* (a Classical Yoga text dated in a range from the third century BCE [Before the Common Era] to the third century CE [Common Era]). Sutra means "thread" in Sanskrit and the word refers to a condensed form of the teaching designed for contemplation. The short aphorisms or sutras are reminders of deeper truths revealed from within the seeker's own awakened consciousness. The core of this truth teaching is timeless and unchangeable. Patanjali's *Yoga Sutra* is a complex, highly technical work, which invites a lifetime of study and practice. This book attempts to make these ancient teachings more accessible by providing examples appropriate to our current age. For this reason, I have taken some liberties with the interpretation of the sutras, suggesting applications to situations in our daily life that far exceed any of Patanjali's original meaning. However, the intention—that of providing a framework for the awakening process—remains unaltered. These time-tested teachings of Self-realization promise that liberation of consciousness is possible in this lifetime. With this liberation comes the experience of authentic being and freedom from suffering.

The Fourfold Practice of Kriya Yoga provides an integrated approach to the awakening process, addressing soul, heart, mind, and right action in the world for seekers today. This work does not intend to be a scholarly treatise on yoga philosophy. It is hoped that those whose deep curiosity to know the Truth is sparked by this effort will pursue their study of the yogic science of Self-realization through the many fine scholarly commentaries available on the *Yoga Sutra*.

This book evolved from handouts for the spiritual practice courses I have been teaching for nearly a decade, first as a workbook, then to its present form with the assistance of students, friends, and colleagues. I am grateful to Anne Cawley who provided the inspiration and support for the first workbook and paved the way for this book. For encouragement and professional support with the artwork and editing I thank Amy Sibiga, Clarice Hirata, and Judith Pynn. For having faith in the project and in me, I thank my husband Michael Scott. And I extend my appreciation to the many dedicated students at the Center for Spiritual Enlightenment who have taken the course over the years and put the teachings into practice.

The Center for Spiritual Enlightenment is a spiritual teaching center in San Jose, California founded in 1981. The ministry of the Center is focused on the essential truth and harmony found in the world's religions, the necessity for a global ethical and spiritual awakening, and the importance of individual participation toward this goal. Our vision is individual and planetary awakening to the One Truth known by many names. The Center today carries on the work of bridging the teachings of the East and the West while providing a place for those who seek to practice the Eternal Way, the sacred truths found at the core of all religions.

The spiritual teaching of the Center may be experienced through many different avenues. The Center offers worship services, adult education classes in spiritual philosophy, practice, and healthy living, hatha yoga, retreats, spiritual direction and counseling, children's spiritual education, spiritual community, and leadership training. At the World Headquarters one will find the Temple of the Eternal Way, a sanctuary of worship, meditation gardens, adult education class-rooms, Children's Spiritual Education Center, the Love in Action Ministry School for ordained ministry, a space for yoga practice, a meditation chapel, and administrative offices.

This book is intended to be used as a workbook for engaged spiritual practice—for testing the spiritual principles in the laboratory of everyday life experience. To live authentically, one must find a way to unfetter the soul—to quiet the mind, clear away false belief, and allow the soul expression in daily life experience. This spiritual training course offers a spiritual philosophy and practice in harmony with the essential components of the Eternal Way. The inner way of meditation, contemplation, and prayer is combined with the way of selfless service and right action in the world. Balancing the inner, devotional nature with the outer expression of enlightened activity brings serenity of mind. The cultivation of this serenity allows one to develop the ability to attune to inner wisdom and soul guidance, thus living an awakened life in harmony with Spirit. The authentic, awakened life promises a true freedom and joy quite unlike anything the satisfaction of desires in the material world alone has to offer. An ease of being, a Self-sustaining sense of fulfillment, and unconditional love are waiting your discovery.

Namasté—Reverence to the Divine within you,
Reverend Ellen Grace O'Brian
Fall 1998

Part One
The Eternal Way

Mother you have shown the doves
where and how to build their nests
in the temple eaves.
I am a lost one,
the generation
who did not learn to sew,
the recipes of my grandmothers
are gone.
I left that house.
Now you
must show me
the simple
weaving together
of the soul life.

—Ellen Grace O'Brian,
The Sanctuary of Belonging

One
Beginnings

Lead me from the unreal to the Real.
Lead me from ignorance to light.
Lead me from death to immortality.
—Brihad-aranyaka Upanishad 1.3.28

"Seek and you will find"…"Knock and the door will open"…These familiar words of encouragement have been spoken through the ages in various ways by spiritually awake individuals. Those who have experienced the full potential of spiritual realization reveal to seekers of truth the accessibility and the nearness of enlightenment. "The kingdom/queendom of heaven is within you…" "The Tao is hidden but always present…" Shining like precious gems hidden in a cave, the priceless treasure of spiritual wisdom awaits our discovery.

The "cave" holding the precious gems is our own consciousness. The shining gems represent one's own soul wisdom that shines with the light of Spirit or Supreme Consciousness. Each soul is an individualized unit of Supreme Consciousness, and like shining facets of a diamond, each facet catches the light and reflects it in a unique way. As individualized expressions of the One Life of Spirit, we are at the same time one with the Source and unique expressions of Its infinite creative expression.

Each soul reflects the light of Supreme Consciousness in a unique way.

Through our connection to the Source of All, each of us is wealthy beyond our greatest imaginings. Within our own consciousness is the precious gem of our true nature. This true nature, our soul nature, contains within it the qualities and potentials of Spirit: eternal being, infinite consciousness, and creative power. All needs can be met through our spiritual resources. All pain can be healed. We can enjoy infinite abundance. It is possible for us to know unshakable contentment and unconditional love.

The Journey Home

Spiritual realization is the direct experience of one's divine Self.

The spiritual path of Self-realization is really a journey "home" to the experience of one's own true nature. Dispassion (or faith) and self-discipline (right action or soul-inspired action) provide the nutrients for the seed of realization which already exists within us to bloom. This blooming is the natural unfolding of one's essential spiritual nature. Nothing is changed at the soul level. Nothing is added on. One has simply journeyed home to the exquisite flowering of the Divine in and as one's own Self. This is perhaps the strangest paradox of all: why do we need to enter a path, to travel nowhere, to discover that which we already have?

If we accept that we are already spiritual in nature, it naturally follows that realization of this truth of who we are is not created by some outside force, but rather revealed from the inner core of our own knowing. Spiritual realization is the direct experience of one's divine Self. The ability of human beings to experience their own divine nature directly is obscured by various factors. So experience of the Divine, although potentially accessible to every human being, is not easily or readily perceived. Following the spiritual path, the Eternal Way, opens the doors of perception.

The Eternal Way

One God, One Life, One Reality exists.

In 1893 a bright star appeared on the horizon of American religious thought, and many Americans were receptive to the light. In September of that year, Swami Vivekananda arrived from India to speak at the World Parliament of Religions in Chicago, bringing with him the spiritual philosophy of the Eternal Way, universal spiritual teachings based on the Vedas, the sacred mystical scriptures of Hinduism. The philosophy he carried spoke of the One Reality of God and all of life, the harmony of science and religion, the innate goodness of human beings, the belief in the direct accessibility of Divine Reality to humans, and significantly, a technology to access this Reality. The sense of universality that the Eternal Way represents was particularly attractive to the American religious spirit: all true religions are seen as different paths converging upon the same goal—Self- or God-realization.

Some of the essential philosophical ideas of the Eternal Way were already making their way into American thought when Vivekananda arrived. The Transcendentalists, particularly Emerson and Thoreau, had been inspired by the wisdom of the scriptures from the East and had put forth the idea that the knowledge of Reality is available intuitively. Sir Edwin Arnold composed *The Song Celestial*, an English rendition of the Hindu scripture the *Bhagavad Gita*, which became available in 1885 and reached an audience thirsty for its teachings. It was also the time of the emergence of America's new metaphysical religions—Theosophy, Christian Science, and the New Thought movement—which offered a philosophical approach to spirituality similar to Vedanta (the teachings of the Vedas). Another great teacher from India, Paramahansa Yogananda, traveled to the U.S. in 1920 and lectured at the International Congress of Religious Liberals sponsored by the American Unitarian Association. The great yogi saint Mahavatar Babaji had many years earlier predicted Yogananda's journey to America. He and Yogananda's guru, Sri Yukteswar, met at the Kumbha Mela religious festival in Allahabad, India in 1894. Babaji told Sri Yukteswar he would send him a disciple who would carry the teachings of yoga to the West and contribute to the harmonious interchange between the East and the West. In fact, Yogananda remained in the United States for a time, journeying across the country on a speaking tour. Crowds of thousands came to hear him. Headquarters were established in Los Angeles for Yogananda's organization, Self-Realization Fellowship. During his lifetime Yogananda drew many souls to the path of God-realization, and the impact of his presence continues to this day.

In 1944 Aldous Huxley, who was influenced by Vedanta, would write his classic spiritual anthology, *The Perennial Philosophy*. Huxley states that his work presents "the metaphysic that recognizes a divine Reality substantial to the world of things and lives and minds; the psychology that finds in the soul something similar to, or even identical with, divine Reality." Huxley noted that this Perennial Philosophy was to be found in the traditions of early peoples in every region of the world and exists in the mystical core of all the world's

Knowledge of Reality is available intuitively.

religions. Today the terms Perennial Philosophy, Eternal Religion, or Eternal Way refer to the mystical strand of truth teaching that runs through all sacred traditions.

The name "Eternal Way" is a translation of the Sanskrit term "Sanatana Dharma." Dharma is the way of harmony with one's own divine true Self—the way of righteousness, spiritual law, or truth. The Eternal Way signifies the spiritual philosophy and practice that leads one from the human condition of confusion and unknowingness to spiritual awakening and a life in harmony with the Divine. While the scriptural origins of this philosophy are identified in the sacred teachings of Hinduism, the essence of the Eternal Way itself is not a religion. It is the eternal path of spiritual awakening for all people in all times.

THE FOUR PRINCIPLES

The spiritual philosophy of the Eternal Way posits four essential principles on the path of spiritual awakening. These principles can be found in all spiritual traditions at the depth level of the teachings. While each religion or spiritual teaching has its cultural differences and significant variations in belief systems and practices, the Eternal Way brings in to focus what is called the "golden thread of truth," the harmony of esoteric wisdom that is universal to the human spiritual experience. The teaching of the Eternal Way reveals that these universal truths have been experienced throughout time by people from diverse cultures and traditions in profoundly similar ways. While the language to describe the experience or the cultural mores surrounding it may differ, what remains essentially the same is the universal human spiritual experience of awakening from delusion to truth, from the bondage of identification with the false self to the freedom of knowing the true Self. The spiritual path offers the way to embark upon this journey of Self-discovery.

The Eternal Way is the spiritual experience at the core of the world's religions.

The four basic principles of the Eternal Way are:

There are four basic principles of the Eternal Way.

1. Supreme Consciousness or Spirit is the single Reality out of which all else proceeds. There is nothing that exists without Spirit, or that is separate from the Creator.

2. Human beings are an extension of this single Reality and therefore have the inherent ability to experience It directly.

3. Human beings are comprised of the dual nature of Spirit and matter (or nature). When in the world, people identify themselves with the physical body and mind and so are subject to forgetting their essential nature as spiritual.

4. Through the practice of self-discipline and the influence of divine grace, it is possible for human beings to awaken to or remember their true nature as spiritual beings. This is the purpose of life.

These four principles can be "condensed" in the following way and committed to memory, as a useful tool of study:

1 It is.

2. We are It.

3. We forget.

4. We remember.

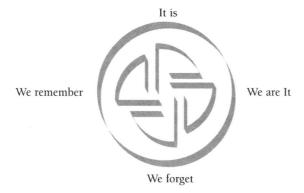

The Purpose and Practice of Living the Eternal Way

The purpose of living the Eternal Way as it has been lived through the centuries is the liberation of consciousness, or finding freedom in the true Self. The science of yoga evolved from the Eternal Way philosophy as its method of practical application.

The word yoga is derived from the Sanskrit root, meaning "to yoke" or "bind back." This term yoga translated as "to bind back" signifies union with the divine Self, the return to or complete remembrance of our original identity. Contained in the meaning of the word "yoke" is the full sense of discipline required to train the mind, as one would yoke an ox. What once wandered aimlessly is harnessed for higher purposes.

The philosophy and practice of yoga is a significant aspect of the spiritual heritage of human beings, reflecting the primary essence of human spiritual experience. It is based upon Vedic wisdom representing thousands of years of inquiry into the nature of reality, the practice of self-discipline, and devotion. The original Vedic seers were practitioners of spiritual science thousands of years ago who directed their attention inward to discern the truth about life. Their revelations were originally transmitted orally and later committed to writing. The body of sacred texts containing this teaching is known as the Vedas. The word "Vedas" means knowledge, wisdom, vision, or revealed truth.

The Vedas are the basis of the revelatory teachings of Hinduism. However, because of their complexity, diversity, and scope they are not considered the primary scripture for any particular sect of Hinduism but rather the well from which their scriptural wisdom is drawn.

The Vedas are a collection of wisdom pertaining to spiritual revelation. Sections of the Vedas include hymns (mantra), ritualistic teachings, theological teachings, and philosophical treatises. The Rig Veda is considered to be the most ancient of the Vedas. It is thought to originate anywhere from 4000 BCE to as early as 12,000 BCE and is the oldest book in Sanskrit or any Indo-European language. The compilation of the Vedas is thought to have occurred around 1500 BCE.

Yoga is the science of spiritual awakening as it has been revealed throughout time. The purpose of yoga is to experience Self-realization, the truth of one's being which removes suffering and makes it possible to dwell in the natural bliss of the soul. A spiritual path rather than a religion, yoga is a practice that can be appreciated by seekers of all faiths and traditions who are seeking Self-realization.

"Yoga" signifies union with the divine Self, the return to our original identity.

The One Truth the sages call by many names.
—Rig Veda I.164

Through the disciplines of the yoga path the aspirant gains entrance to the "kingdom/queendom," the true Self within, and is freed from the tyranny of the reactive patterns of the ego self. Thus has yoga been called the discipline of freedom, and yoga philosophy has been called the science of Self-realization.

PREPARING THE WAY

Throughout the course, you will be writing down your experiences, thoughts, insights, and remembrances. Use the space provided or a separate notebook. In either case, you may want to have a record of your journey.

1. Reflect on your feelings about beginning this course now. Write about any concerns or hopes that you have as you begin.

   What are your intentions or goals for engaging in this spiritual practice?

2. Review the four principles of the Eternal Way. Write about your understanding of the four principles.

   •

   •

   •

   •

It is

We remember

We are It

We forget

3. Have you experienced the cycle of forgetting/remembering in your spiritual journey? Write about your experience including the factors you feel influenced your process of "forgetting" as well as your process of "remembering."

Sometimes a man humbles himself in his heart, submits the visible to the power to see, and seeks to return to his source. He seeks, he finds, and he returns home…To return to the source of things, one has to travel in the opposite direction…

—Rene Daumal

The Self is the light:

The light is covered by darkness:

This darkness is delusion:

That is why we dream.

When the light of the Self

Drives out our darkness

That light shines forth from us,

A sun in splendor,

Spirit revealed.

—*Bhagavad Gita 5:15-16*
(adapted from trans. by
Prabhavananda)

Two
The Paths of Awakening

INTRODUCTION TO YOGA

Yoga is the method of practice in which the truth of the precepts of the Eternal Way is directly verified. In yoga, it is considered essential that one have direct experience of the teaching. The goal is for one to become liberated or Self-realized. Self-realization occurs through the direct perception of soul knowledge. This direct perception cannot be attained from reading books. Neither is it created through the practice of spiritual exercises; they only prepare the way. This truth already exists within the soul, so it cannot be attained or created. It can only be remembered. The various ways of yoga support this goal by helping the seeker to create an environment conducive to the experience of awakening.

Yoga is the way for one to explore the teaching within the realm of direct, personal experience.

Root Associations

The word "yoga" itself refers to union through its root meaning "to bind, or to yoke." The sense of the term "to bind back" describes the intention of yoga to assist seekers in reuniting with the knowledge and experience of their original nature. Through identification with the mind and senses, human beings become lost in the world, forgetting their true nature as Spirit. The "binding back" indicates a return in consciousness to one's home, to one's true Self.

The word yoga also has within its root associations a meaning akin to the word "sacrifice." The self-discipline required in the practice of yoga is a sacrifice of the highest order. The devotee offers the

The sacrifice of yoga is a continual letting go of whatever obscures the true Self.

"work" of their path of awakening as a sacrifice upon the altar of awakening to the true Self. The perceptions and limitations of the ego-bound self are sacrificed to the higher, innate divine perspective. The sacrifice of yoga is a continual letting go of whatever obscures the true Self. This process of letting go ultimately allows the devotee to discover his or her essential union with the Divine, or Supreme Consciousness.

Many branches of yoga developed over time, becoming a technology of divine discovery. At times, the teachings of these branches may seem contradictory. For example, one branch of yoga philosophy may recommend meditation or contemplation as a way, while another recommends being actively involved in service. One must look to the purpose of these disciplines; there the essential unity of the message will be found.

The essential unity of various branches of yoga is found in the purpose of each discipline.

The branches of yoga, like the various disciplines of different religions, arose out of the needs of different temperaments of human beings. Some people are more naturally contemplative, others tend toward activity. Since people are holistic, complex beings, the practices that developed according to temperament type overlap in their definitions and practice.

Yoga of Technique

In the West, the word yoga is often associated with the practice of Hatha Yoga, commonly misunderstood to be only a type of physical exercise. Hatha is one type of yoga, part of the branch of what is called the Yoga of Technique.

The yoga of technique helps the seeker to clear obstacles in the body/mind to the clear perception of the soul.

The branch of yoga that encourages the practice of techniques is aimed at helping the seeker remove obstacles to the clear perception of the soul. Kundalini Yoga, Laya Yoga, and Kriya Yoga as well as Hatha Yoga may be placed under this umbrella. Kundalini Yoga focuses attention on techniques to awaken the dormant vital force of energy within the body/mind, thereby removing obstacles to clear perception. Laya (or Nada) Yoga is a practice geared toward realization through meditation upon and contemplation of the inner sound, the Aum. Kriya Yoga is mentioned in the *Yoga Sutra* as defining the four essential practices of yoga: surrender of the sense of separate existence, meditation, study of the nature of consciousness (contemplation), and self-discipline (cultivating the virtues). The word "kriya" means both action and purification. It is through the practice of all the various yoga techniques that one purifies the body and mind, making it a clear vehicle for divine perception.

Hatha Yoga is an engaged practice, meaning "mindful or conscious," which uses the body/mind as the primary vehicle. The postures practiced are designed to bring balance to the flow of energy in the body and thus contribute to mental clarity. When the body/mind is in perfect balance, the soul nature or oneness with the divine Self can be experienced. With regard to the yogas mentioned in the category of technique, it should be understood that technique is rightly practiced only to facilitate surrender to the higher Self. Technique as an end in itself is not in harmony with the purpose of yoga. What one seeks to experience is beyond the realm of nature, body, or mind. It cannot be created through technique. Technique is only practiced to cleanse the doors of perception.

In the opening verses of the classic text on Hatha Yoga, the *Hatha-Yoga-pradipika* (written by Svatmarama Yogendra in the mid-fourteenth century CE) Svatmarama says, "I salute the Lord Siva who taught Parvati the science of Hatha Yoga, which is the stairway for those who wish to attain the lofty Raja Yoga." In the second verse he maintains that the practice of Hatha Yoga is solely for the attainment of Raja Yoga.

Bhakti Yoga

Bhakti is the yoga of love and devotion. Through the practice of continually offering the focus of one's heart to the indwelling Presence, one experiences union. Chanting, singing to God, prayer, ritual offerings, and seeing and loving Divine Presence in all are tools of Bhakti Yoga.

Through the practice of love and devotion to the indwelling Presence, one experiences union.

The focus on worshipping God through love, as Divine Beloved, may be placed upon an image of the Divine, upon an incarnation of the Divine (an avatar or a saint), or upon one's spiritual teacher. This mode of loving the sacred "other" is ultimately intended to assist seekers in discovering the indwelling Divine Beloved—the essence of Love that dwells within their own heart, and is their own true nature. Paramahansa Yogananda and Sri Ramakrishna are examples of bhakti yogins. In all religions, one can find bhakti yogins, those whose spiritual practice is their love for God.

Karma Yoga

Karma Yoga is the way of selfless service. In this practice one is actively involved in serving God, but surrenders all the "fruits" or results of the service to the Divine, eliminating attachment to the outcome of actions. All work is done as worship of the Divine.

One is active only for the sake of awakening and attaining liberation of consciousness.

Through Karma Yoga one surrenders all desire for personal gain and is active only for the sake of awakening and attaining liberation of consciousness. Therefore all action is undertaken in the spirit of renunciation.

It is taught that the only actions in this world that are non-binding (do not create karmic patterns to later be worked out) are those that are fully surrendered to Spirit. As with the other yogas, the goal remains the same: realization of the divine Self. As one surrenders all action to the Divine, eventually one merges the sense of separate existence into the allness of Spirit. All action is then done by, for, and through Spirit. Mahatma Gandhi and His Holiness the Dalai Lama are examples of a life of Karma Yoga.

Sometimes the practices of Bhakti and Karma Yoga intersect. As one loves God, there is a tendency to then be engaged in serving God. Mother Teresa of Calcutta would be an example of a bhakti (one who focused on her love for her Divine Beloved Jesus) who went about serving Jesus in all.

Jnana Yoga

Study, contemplation, meditation, and inquiry are tools for the path of Jnana Yoga.

Jnana Yoga is the yoga of wisdom or discernment in which one uses the faculty of awakened intelligence to experience the truth. Study, contemplation, meditation, and inquiry are tools that develop the ability to discern. The focus upon knowledge is Self-knowledge, not knowledge as can be acquired from gathering external information. The perception of the Self occurs beyond the thinking mind. The jnana yogin seeks to make the distinction between Pure Consciousness which is unchanging, thoughts which arise in the mind, and the thinking mind itself. One practicing Jnana Yoga might inquire within, seeking illumination, with a simple yet profound question such as: Who am I? As one observes from the steady witness consciousness the changing nature of the body, of thought, and emotion, one begins to discern that the true nature is not that. The

Indian sage Ramana Maharshi is an example of a jnana yogin. Ken Wilbur with his combination of research and personal exploration into the spectrum of consciousness may be considered to be a modern day jnana yogin.

Raja Yoga

Raja Yoga means the "royal way" and is believed by some to have been the practice of kings or royalty. This path stresses an integrated approach bringing together study, meditation, surrendered devotion, and the practice of self-discipline. All of the other yogas—the yogas of technique as well as Bhakti, Karma, and Jnana—are combined in the practice of Raja Yoga.

The *Yoga Sutra* of Patanjali is the principal text for defining the practice of Raja Yoga, also called Ashtanga Yoga (Eight-Limbed Yoga), Classical Yoga, or Kriya Yoga. These different names all refer to the same branch of yoga but each term carries a slightly different emphasis. Use of the term Raja Yoga emphasizes integration of the major yoga paths. The term Kriya Yoga also signifies integration with a focus on purification. When this yoga is referred to as Ashtanga Yoga (Eight-Limbed Yoga), the eight limbs or means of practice outlined by Patanjali in the *Yoga Sutra* are the focus. Classical Yoga is a term used to denote Patanjali's philosophy as belonging to the dualist school since he distinguishes between Spirit and matter.

Kriya Yoga

The principal path of yoga delineated in the *Yoga Sutra* is Kriya Yoga. The word "Kriya" signifies action, purification, or sanctification. Some have identified Kriya Yoga as a yoga purely of technique, but when the philosophy is understood, one sees that Kriya Yoga is comprehensive and rightly belongs in the category of Raja Yoga. The Kriya path is a way of life. It is a way to sanctify one's life through four essential disciplines—contemplation, meditation, cultivation of the virtues, and surrender of the sense of separate existence. These four disciplines of Kriya Yoga are referred to in this text as the Fourfold Practice of Kriya Yoga.

Patanjali (beyond the name, nothing is known of this sage) compiled the *Yoga Sutra* from the Vedic body of yogic wisdom around

Kriya Yoga is a way of life—a way to sanctify one's life.

200 CE. (There is considerable scholarly debate as to the precise dating of this work). The word "sutra" means thread, a concise reminder of a vast body of holy wisdom. Imagine how a single thread connects to the complex pattern within a tapestry; this is how inner wisdom is woven together in consciousness. Thus the *Yoga Sutra* of Patanjali consists of 195 concise aphorisms called "sutras," which connect to vast reservoirs of inner knowledge. These 195 sutras are usually referred to with the singular term *"Yoga Sutra"* which emphasizes the entire body of work and its significance as a primary source of yoga philosophy. One is urged to study these sutras through deep and prayerful contemplation, to stir the soul memory of Divine realization.

The four sections of the *Yoga Sutra* are: the cultivation of pure awareness, the path or way including the eight limbs of practice, soul powers, and spiritual liberation.

The Eight Limbs of Practice

Be still, and know that I am God.
—Psalm 46:10

In the second section of the *Yoga Sutra*, Patanjali introduces the eight limbs or means for accomplishing the cessation of thought activity and experiencing pure awareness. The eight limbs (or components of practice) are:

1. The Restraints (Yamas): Harmlessness, Truthfulness, Non-Stealing, Right Use of Vital Force, and Non-Attachment

2. The Observances (Niyamas): Cleanliness, Contentment, Self-Discipline, Study of the Nature of Consciousness, and Surrender of the Sense of Separateness

3. Posture (Asana)

4. Control of Vital Force (Pranayama)

5. Interiorization (Pratyahara)

6. Concentration (Dharana)

7. Meditation (Dhyana)

8. Oneness (Samadhi)

The "limbs" provide a structure for combining the practice of meditation and the cultivation of the virtues. In this text the following restraints and observances—harmlessness, truthfulness, non-stealing, right use of vital force, non-attachment, cleanliness, contentment, and self-discipline—are covered in Part Two, Chapter Seven, Cultivating the Virtues. Study of the nature of consciousness is addressed in Part Two, Chapter Five, Contemplation. Posture, control of vital force, interiorization, concentration, and meditation comprise Chapter Six in Part Two, Meditation and Prayer. Surrender of the sense of separateness is the focus of the concluding chapter in Part Two, Chapter Eight, Surrender and Service.

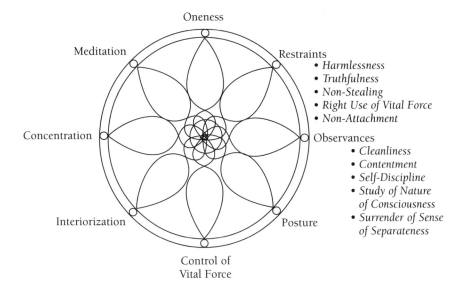

A systematic approach to God-realization brings forth the inner experience that fuels the devotee's ability to make real change. One must touch the depths of truth, the awareness of one's divine nature, in meditation. This experience of knowing the truth of who we are provides the sustaining motivation for changing our life. To try to live a virtuous life without inner realization is like trying to build a beautiful home without a foundation. It is hard work and is easily broken down in times of crisis. The combination of meditation and cultivation of the virtues brings stability.

PREPARING THE WAY

1. Find examples in modern day life of individuals who exemplify the different approaches to yoga.
   • Hatha Yoga:
   • Bhakti Yoga:
   • Karma Yoga:
   • Jnana Yoga:
   • Raja Yoga:

2. Find a photo of an individual who exemplifies the ideals of yoga to you and place it where it can be an uplifting reminder to you of the Way.

3. Consider your own temperament type as it is expressed in worship. What forms of worship most interest you?

   What forms of worship least interest you?

   Is it possible that the area of worship of least interest to you is an aspect of your self in need of greater integration?

4. Consider your practice and worship. Many scriptures teach that it is the quality of the intention, or the heart of the seeker, that is valuable beyond any particular ritual or practice.

   What brings heart and purity of intention to your practice?

One who wants to expand
the field of happiness, must
lay the foundation of it on
the bottom of the heart.

—*Tract of the Quiet Way*

Three
The Fourfold Practice of Kriya Yoga

Self-discipline, meditation and the study of sacred scripture, and complete dedication to God constitute the path of Kriya Yoga.

—*Yoga Sutra II.1*

In the opening verse of the second chapter of the *Yoga Sutra*, Patanjali outlines the essential components of the practice of Kriya Yoga as the method for cultivating pure awareness. These four main elements of the Kriya Yoga system provide the foundation for the depth work of dismantling the false self, transforming the personality, and revealing the true Self, the spiritual essence of being.

Most commentaries on the *Yoga Sutra* emphasize three primary techniques—aestheticism, study, and devotion or surrender—as the core of Patanjali's Kriya Yoga system. This text identifies the practice of meditation as the fourth essential element, since the fundamental emphasis of the Kriya path is the attainment of meditative awareness and a significant portion of the text is devoted to meditation instruction. The practice of meditation is inseparable from true study (contemplation), self-discipline, and devotion. When the pure intention of each of these practices is completely fulfilled, the result is meditative awareness. For the sake of emphasizing the importance of meditation as a key element of the practice, this text describes Kriya Yoga as "the Fourfold Practice."

The Fourfold Practice of Kriya Yoga consists of these core practices:

1. Study/Contemplation
2. Meditation/Prayer
3. Self-discipline/Cultivating the Virtues
4. Dedication to God/Surrender and Service

CONTEMPLATION

From the spiritual perspective, the source of all suffering is ignorance—not ignorance of worldly knowledge, but of Spirit. Through contemplation, the study of the nature of consciousness, one seeks to know the truth and to be free from this suffering born of ignorance. Fear and suffering are the result of superimposing a sense of reality on that which is unreal, and assuming the unreal to be real. Through various mistaken assumptions, human beings identify themselves with the body and with the contents of the mind, assuming this to be their real identity. Both the body and mind are continually subject to change. Therefore, they cannot be one's true, or lasting identity. Only the spiritual essence, that which is beyond changing phenomena, can be considered Real, in the absolute sense.

The only cure for ignorance is knowledge— the experience of Self-knowledge.

Identifying with body and mind, human beings become subject to experiencing themselves as an effect of the fluctuations of the contents of the mind. This brings about the experiences of pleasure or pain depending upon the type and origin of the particular mental activity. Being subject to the effects of this unstable identity rather than rooted in Absolute Truth is ignorance.

The only cure for this ignorance is knowledge—not the accumulation of information but the experience of Self-knowledge, realization of the Truth of one's being. This knowledge is accessible through experience because it is the core of one's own existence. A recovery of one's authentic Self comes about through a shift in identity. When one no longer identifies with the body/mind, the true Self is revealed.

Study of the nature of consciousness is an essential aspect of the path of awakening. It is pursued through a careful study of scripture, such as the *Yoga Sutra*, combined with the practice of contemplation, or self-inquiry. This book focuses primarily on the teachings presented in the *Yoga Sutra*, but any true scripture is a valid source of study. The *Torah*, the New Testament of the *Bible*, the *Koran*, the *Tao Te Ching*, the *Bhagavad Gita*, the *Dhammapada*, and many others are reservoirs of sacred knowledge.

The scriptures and the writings of awakened sages carry within them the conscious realization of the adept. Through studying enlightened works, a seeker shares in the consciousness of the writer. Truth, in spoken or written form, carries the power to change us by awakening our own latent soul knowledge.

The ancient spiritual languages such as Sanskrit, Hebrew, and Latin contain their meanings within the resonance of the words themselves. This is why chanting of various scriptures is an important aspect of study. The sound energy of the scripture has an uplifting influence on the consciousness of the speaker and listener, literally resonating the energy of the speaker with the Creator/Source.

Careful and committed study of scripture is combined with inquiry into one's own perceptions of the nature of reality and the Self.

Careful and committed study of scripture is combined with inquiry into one's own perceptions of the nature of reality and the Self. Scripture is not merely read, but contemplated and taken in to be explored in the experience of the reader. Self-study may also take the form of the profoundly simple inquiry such as asking "who am I?" In asking this the seeker observes the changing nature of thoughts, feelings, and phenomena with an intention to see clearly the nature of the true Self.

MEDITATION AND PRAYER

Learning to focus and to concentrate on a single point of attention is the essential preparatory stage of meditation which later facilitates one's ability to be inwardly attentive, aware of inner guidance and altered states of consciousness. The practice of meditation is likely the most significant tool available to spiritual seekers. As this skill is developed, one becomes capable of distinguishing thought, volition, intuition, and the silence of the essential Self.

Meditation: flowing one's attention to the pure, unchanging aspect of consciousness.

Meditation can be defined as flowing one's attention to the pure, unchanging aspect of consciousness. When meditation has stabilized, one can move more deeply into inner, mystical experiences of the divine nature. The stages of meditative absorption are preliminary to ecstatic, mystical experiences. One does not create these experiences through the practice of meditation but rather, through meditation, becomes receptive to them.

Prayer is communing with the divine Self. While it has many forms, the key ingredient of prayer is surrendered devotion which opens the heart and mind to the influx of creative energy from the Source. Those researching the potential effects of prayer have validated that positive changes occur regardless of the type of prayer. What matters is that we pray, not how we pray. For the bhakti yogin, talking to God is a natural expression of their devotional nature. The jnana yogins are more likely to pray by acknowledging the allness of the divine Self and opening to Its influence. Understanding and respecting our own spiritual temperament allows us to pray in a way that has heart and meaning for us. True devotion is an authentic expression of the self that awakens divine potential. Devotion itself does not cause awakening but is significant to opening one's heart and mind to the possibility.

Here is where grace enters in. Grace may be thought of as the uplifting aspect of Divine Consciousness that moves in and through human beings, drawing us ever nearer to Itself through love. The devotee, through prayer and meditation, prepares the inner environment. Through grace, divine insight is given.

The *Yoga Sutra* contains precise instruction for meditation itself, and offers guidelines for creating optimum conditions through a righteous lifestyle. As one practices meditation, the changes one needs to make in order to live the spiritual life become clearer.

It also becomes clearer that one is not able to accomplish the depth of change necessary through will power and self-discipline alone. Divine intervention is needed, or the direct assistance of one's higher Consciousness. Prayer thus becomes a significant part of one's practice. Through the discipline learned in meditation, it is possible to eventually learn to "pray without ceasing." The saints of many traditions prayed in this way—living in the world but not of it—their hearts and minds continually absorbed in divine recollection.

The devotee, through prayer and meditation, prepares the inner environment. Through grace, divine insight is given.

Cultivating the Virtues

The *Yoga Sutra* teaches certain universal values found in all the great spiritual traditions. The cultivation of the values of harmlessness, truthfulness, non-stealing, right action, non-attachment, cleanliness, and contentment all contribute to our spiritual development by prompting us to become ever more conscious of our actions in the world. As we explore how our thoughts and behaviors affect ourselves and others, we can move beyond conditioned reactions to conscious choices that are in harmony with the divine influence.

The cultivation of the virtues works in harmony with the practice of meditation. Meditation assists with the quieting of the mind which allows us to become more aware of the motives and tendencies involved in our choices and actions. We begin to see more clearly why we do what we do.

The cultivation of the virtues works in harmony with the practice of meditation.

When there is conflict between one's lifestyle and the knowing of the soul, the devotee finds meditation difficult. The conflict produces unrest in the mental field, thwarting clear focus and access to the serenity of the soul. This becomes a signal to make the changes necessary to bring one's lifestyle into integrity. Cultivation of the virtues contributes to the conscious alignment of activity and thought with the soul nature.

This text explores the cultivation of the virtues in relationship to life in contemporary society. There are suggestions in this work (such as pondering the use of credit cards) that are specific to this time and which invite expansion of Patanjali's treatise. Given the difference in culture and time, it is the intention of this work to make the basic concepts of yoga more widely applicable and available.

The spiritual practices of self-discipline and cultivating the virtues have often been associated with strong asceticism. Just the sound of the phrase has been known to frighten seekers, to send them off searching for that easier, softer way! For many people, especially those in the more developed nations who have grown accustomed to instant gratification, having what we want when we want it, self-discipline has a ring of "deprivation" to it. This is especially true when it comes to putting a limit on the gratification of desires. Materialistic cultures are built upon the constant creation and gratification of consumer desires, and we often feel entitled to indulge these desires in "pursuit of happiness."

Self-discipline loosens the hold of many assumptions about the way we live. It invites us to consider what is in greatest harmony with our soul—to be inwardly, rather than outwardly, directed.

Spiritual self-discipline is following the deepest urges of one's own inner Self. This is the key to understanding the true nature of self-discipline. It is not the asceticism that some imagine as torturing one's self to conform to outer standards by the constraint of will power. It is doing what is most in harmony with, and most serves the expression of, the soul nature, and therefore, is very nurturing to the individual.

Today more than ever, an integrated approach to spirituality is needed so that spiritual practice is not something apart from daily life, but becomes the essential value out of which all else proceeds. In order to halt the destruction of our planet, it is imperative that we begin to heal ourselves. In order to heal ourselves, to become "whole," we are challenged to live each day consciously in this world. Every moment of every day we are walking upon the spiritual path. Nothing, no circumstance, activity, or relationship in our life exists outside of our spiritual path. This recognition invites divine grace into our lives and helps us evolve to seeing that all of life is, indeed, sacred.

Every moment of every day we are walking upon the spiritual path.

SURRENDER AND SERVICE

The fourth essential practice on this path is that of surrender. Spiritual surrender is the process of letting go of attachment to one's ego identification. It is letting go of our insistence on being a separate self and allowing ourselves to experience our connection with the Divine. Surrender, then, is releasing whatever obscures our ability to perceive our true nature. A popular saying describes surrender this way: "Let go and let God."

Usually the first question that arises for the devotee upon hearing the instruction to "surrender" is "how?" The clearing away of obstacles to our ability to perceive the true Self is accomplished through all of the disciplines combined: contemplation, meditation and prayer, and cultivation of the virtues. The vision of the Truth of who we are culminates in a life of surrender and spiritual service.

Let go and let God.

Once one is spiritually awake, the natural tendency is to be of service. Understanding that any harmful acts we do in this world we do to ourselves, we refrain from harming. Taking that insight further we also realize that in serving others, we serve ourselves. Spiritual service is not motivated by the kind of altruism that says "I" do this for "them." Spiritual service is an expression of recognizing we are all one in God. Helping another is helping myself—not out of fear, but supreme love.

PREPARING THE WAY

1. Yoga and the Fourfold Practice

   In serving others, we serve ourselves.

   What is your current understanding of the word "yoga"?

   Review the four essentials of the Fourfold Practice of Kriya Yoga. Are you currently engaged in any of the four essential disciplines?

   Which is most familiar to you?

   Which is least familiar?

2. Begin your study of the science of Self-realization.

   Study the course materials and see the recommended reading list in the back of this book for suggestions.

3. Pray for guidance as you embark upon this sacred journey.

4. Write a self-discipline inventory.

   Write an inventory of areas of your life or current behaviors that you believe need additional self-discipline.

What has been your experience of self-discipline in the past?

How can you bring forth a new understanding of self-discipline?

5. Review the role of service in your life.

   Are you currently involved in offering service?

   What has been your experience of serving or volunteering in the past?

   What is your vision of being of service?

You have crossed the great ocean;

Why do you halt so near the shore?

Make haste to get on the other side, Gautama;

be careful all the while!

—*Uttaradhyayana Sutra*

Four
Finding the Way

I gave my heart to seek and search.
—Ecclesiastes 1:13

While there are occasional reports of instantaneous enlightenment, for most people spiritual awakening is a gradual process. A spiritual path is a systematic support system for the natural process of awakening to our full potential as human beings. Just as a physical path is a charted way through territory that can lead us to a desired destination, the spiritual path is a map of the way of awakening offered to us by those who have made the inner journey of realization before us. We are fortunate to live in a time when these "maps" of consciousness are readily available to us from many different sources and traditions, allowing us to discover certain basic elements common to traveling all paths of awakening.

A spiritual path is a systematic support system for the natural process of awakening to our full potential as human beings.

BALANCING PHILOSOPHY AND PRACTICE

To facilitate the journey of Self-discovery, a spiritual path must present both philosophy and practice. These two components are essential. The philosophy provides the fundamental suppositions concerning the nature of spirituality. The practice gives the techniques to test the truth of what is offered in the laboratory of one's own experience.

To study the ideas of others without a practice (even if these

The door of the Truth is covered by a golden disc. Open it, O Nourisher!
—*Isha Upanishad*

ideas represent an enlightened teaching) is to miss out on the essential nature of spiritual work. Study without practice can be likened to going into a fine restaurant, studying the menu, and departing before ordering or ever tasting a meal. No matter how much others have said about the delicious food they have eaten there, it will remain outside of the realm of one's own true knowing—without the ability to provide real nourishment.

Some of the disillusionment voiced with traditional, organized religions today has been the inaccessibility of the mystical practice or the experiential elements of the teaching. Without a practice to experience the teaching directly, spiritual aspirants are left with a set of beliefs and dictates they must struggle to follow without having a way to access the inner resources to do so.

Following external dictates with one's mind and will can only go so far, and frequently invites rebellion of the shadow side of the psyche. When the spiritual path includes practices that deepen one's understanding beyond the surface level of gathering information, the learning is holistic, the growth, organic and sure. It includes, through personal experience; the heart, soul, mind, will, and body.

The scales may sometimes be tipped the other way, as in the case of some New Age teachings that focus primarily on one's own experience without the foundation of a time-tested philosophy. Spiritual practice without the discipline of philosophical study tends to increase confusion and to lack the necessary underpinnings for integrating such experiences into one's life.

We live in a time where a literal feast of spiritual teachings are available. In order to fully benefit from this nourishment for the soul, one must choose a path, study it deeply, and participate fully. The study of the philosophical aspect of spiritual teachings provides a foundation for one's experience and realizations. Strong dedication to spiritual practice will build upon that foundation a knowledge that is unshakable. When this stability of spiritual realization is accomplished, an individual can be in the world living free, moment to moment.

The inclination to thrive is inherent to the soul.

WHY WE LOOK FOR A SPIRITUAL PATH

Once survival needs are met, we are inclined to move beyond just meeting needs to discover the secret of thriving. When the dormant desire for spiritual fulfillment is awakened, we must find a path, a way of supporting the process of soul realization.

The reasons people seek a path are many: looking for relief from pain and suffering, seeking wisdom or power, desiring to be of service and to participate in the larger life plan, or desiring a closer relationship with the Divine.

One of the most common motivations leading people to begin to seek spirituality is the desire to be free from pain or suffering. Life as they have known it has proven to be somehow too painful or disappointing. Perhaps they experienced the death of a loved one, the loss of a valued career position, or even just a pervasive feeling of emptiness that asks "is this all there is?" At some point in life, beyond striving to meet survival needs and fulfill various desires, one may begin to question what is truly important.

God is our refuge and strength, a very present help in trouble.
—Psalm 46:1

You may already have an awareness of the deep values that are important to you, but now you are seeking a way to live in harmony with those values. You may be one of the few who seeks out a spiritual way of life in order to fulfill a strong yearning to know and to serve God. If so, you have an advantage on the path.

If all one truly desires is to know and serve God more fully, then each and every event in life is a way to learn, a grist for the mill. For these natural devotees of God, the spiritual path becomes their way of life.

A Lifetime Journey

Whatever one's original motive, embarking upon the spiritual path will introduce a new world of possibility. It holds many surprising turns: times of ease, times of difficulty, and always, new learning and joy. The path is no less than the adventure of a lifetime!

The path is...the adventure of a lifetime!

Although awakening realizations may come quickly, the transformation that follows is a gradual, organic process. With each new realization comes the opportunity to transform the personality self, to allow greater expression of the soul, and to integrate its wisdom into action in one's life.

In one sense, it is an arduous journey. This side of full enlightenment, spiritual growth is never ending. To truly progress requires one's full attention and commitment. Scriptural stories remind us that what is required of us is—everything! Nothing short of our full and

Transformation is a gradual, organic process.

total life commitment will suffice.

A story from the New Testament tells of a young man who has followed the commandments (practiced spiritual self-discipline) for many years. He asks Jesus, "What must I do to inherit eternal life?" Paraphrased, one could ask: What do I need to do to experience full enlightenment? Jesus answers him, "Give up all that you have, and follow me." *What is required is all that you have, your complete commitment to the awakening process.*

Even though we are told that we must give the spiritual path our all, we are assured that we will be given far more in return. Early in the journey, one can discover that spiritual work is Self-nurturing and Self-renewing. Each step of spiritual growth leads us closer to the realization of our own essential nature. As we begin to experience this essential nature of who we are, we are energized. We find fulfillment, a subtle joy that is not found anywhere else. The joy of experiencing one's own soul reality provides the energy and the motivation to continue the spiritual journey.

INGREDIENTS FOR SUCCESS

Dispassion and self-discipline are essential.

The two main ingredients necessary for success on the spiritual path are dispassion and self-discipline. Some would say that there is only one necessary ingredient—love. This may be true, if we consider that love is the essence of life that brings us here and guides us on this journey. However, where love is awakened, one will find dispassion and self-discipline, the two essential components of spiritual commitment.

Dispassion, the ability to be even-minded, non-attached, and non-reactive to circumstances, is the core of faith. Based on one's trust in the true nature of life as spiritual it enables patience and perseverance. Without faith it is too difficult to find our way through the challenges that confront us on the path.

Faith is not a belief one adopts. It is a combination of the inspiration of the heart and direct spiritual experience. Through many experiences of awakening, step by step, faith grows stronger over time. With dedication to the path, one's faith is challenged to expand beyond previous limits.

Self-discipline is action that is taken in harmony with one's deepest wisdom. Rather than an imposed external structure, true self-discipline is learning to follow soul guidance. The practice of self-discipline therefore supports soul realization and our highest happiness.

The techniques and practices of a spiritual devotee are not followed for the sake of the practices themselves or to "be good" but to assist the seeker with the intense discipline that is required to listen and follow direct soul guidance. The combination of dispassion and self-discipline provide the necessary environment in consciousness for realization to occur.

True self-discipline is following soul guidance.

WHY WE LEAVE THE SPIRITUAL PATH

Seekers who come to the path out of desire to find relief from their suffering will often find it after a time of prayer and practice. But a hazard of this particular motivation is that many times when such seekers find relief from what they believe is causing their suffering, they go back to their former way of life and no longer feel a need for spiritual practice. Or, if they do not experience relief from their suffering quickly enough on their chosen path, they may abandon the spiritual way of life altogether.

They may also become compulsive "seekers," looking for help down myriad self-help or metaphysical alleyways, only adding to their original pain and confusion. Usually, after a time, these seekers will return to a balanced path when they are once again sufficiently challenged in life. However, until they become committed to wanting to know the truth about who they are and why they are here, they are likely to bounce back and forth on the path as each surface need is satisfied and each new challenge arises.

Those seeking wisdom or power may experience similar vacillation. When ambitious aspirants find a way to improve their current lifestyle, they often let go of the spiritual focus and put their attention on the fulfillment of desires. Seekers who have been drawn to the path seeking love or money are looking for "more" out of life. After a time of spiritual practice, their attitude and outlook improves, and behold! A new job or a new opportunity arises. The dissatisfaction with their life is gone and off they go in pursuit of even greater happiness. Suddenly the spiritual way of life seems too confining. It requires too much time and sacrifice when it seems there are more interesting or pressing matters to attend to.

*The satisfaction of
desires does not bring
lasting happiness.*

Eventual loss or disappointment in the new found "fix" will usually bring these seekers back. In time, they notice this pattern and become aware that the satisfaction of desires does not bring lasting happiness. Then they will seek to find the true happiness that is only possible through spiritual realization.

OUR DIVINE PURPOSE

Even though we become distracted in the world and lose track of our true nature, always deep within our heart is the call of the true Self, inviting us to remember. Remembering who we are—Self-realization—is the great purpose of life. As we fulfill this purpose of awakening, each of us has a unique and significant part to play in the awakening of the world. Each individual has come into this world with divine purpose, a "blueprint" for their life. There is not one person here who is insignificant to the divine plan. Just as we can observe in nature the unique and essential value of each organism in a living ecosystem, so can we understand the essential value of each person to the living universe. Only when we identify ourselves as limited to mind and body do we feel insignificant to the evolutionary unfolding of the cosmos.

When we begin to awaken to our connection to God, the Supreme Reality, and therefore to our inter-connection to all of life, we begin to sense the significance of this individual lifetime. Why are we here? What is it that the Divine is intending to bring forth as us? Realizing that each person is unique, that no other being will contribute to the cosmic process in exactly the same way, the process of discovering the authentic Self becomes imperative.

To be fully as the Divine intends, it is necessary for each of us to recover our authenticity. The coverings of the false self formulated through mistaken beliefs based on the external constraints of culture or family, or erroneous conclusions made as a result of life experiences, must be removed. In order to see the brightness of the light from a lantern, the glass chimney must be cleared of soot. In order to experience our true Self, that which obscures the expression of the soul must be removed.

*From Joy we come,
in Joy we live, to Joy
we return.*
—*Upanishads*

The exquisite joy of the soul becomes our living reality when the burdens of the false self are removed. Imagine yourself free—living in joy moment to moment. It is our true destiny.

PREPARING THE WAY

Explore the "terrain" of your spiritual path.

Set aside 30 minutes to be alone and quiet.

Gather writing materials and place them nearby to be used following your time of contemplation.

Find a comfortable posture, sitting or even lying down. Take a few deep breaths and with exhalation, let your body relax. Allow your attention to move progressively inward. Simply noticing the rising and falling of your abdomen with your natural breathing rhythm will assist your relaxation and inward focus.

- Once you feel relaxed, allow your mind to review your own journey thus far on the spiritual path.

- What has brought you to this part of the journey now?

- Are there incidents in your life that stand out as particularly significant to your spiritual awakening?

- Were there events, circumstances beyond your control, or individuals that played an important role in your journey?

- Take a moment to appreciate the richness of your journey of awakening so far, and to notice the ways in which you have been supported on the path.

Fear not; for it is God's good pleasure to give you the kingdom.
—Jesus

45

End your time of reflection with a prayer for greater awakening, for the courage to follow your soul guidance each step of the way.

Write down the insights about your spiritual journey that have been revealed to you, noting the particular incidents that you recalled. As you write about your journey, it is likely that more information will surface.

When you have finished writing about your spiritual journey thus far in your life, read over what you have written. Are there any new insights about this journey that surface as you read? Note them on the page as well.

Our birth is but a sleep and a forgetting:

The Soul that rises with us, our life's Star,

Hath had elsewhere its setting,

And cometh from afar:

Not in entire forgetfulness,

And not in utter nakedness,

But trailing clouds of glory do we come.

—William Wordsworth

Part Two
Living the Way

I am the boundless ocean.

This way and that,

The wind, blowing where it will,

Drives the ship of the world.

But I am not shaken.

I am the unbounded deep

In whom the waves of all the worlds

Naturally rise and fall.

But I do not rise or fall.

I am the infinite deep

In whom all the worlds

Appear to rise.

Beyond all form,

Forever still.

Even so am I.

—Ashtavakra Gita

Five
Contemplation

Reality is a level of consciousness, that of non-dual Mind,
containing concepts yet never grasped by them.
—Ken Wilbur, *The Spectrum of Consciousness*

The practice of contemplation or study of the nature of consciousness is one of the four primary components of the Fourfold Practice of Kriya Yoga as well as one of the observances of Eight-Limbed Yoga. Contemplation is experiential inquiry, in which soul knowledge surfaces. In the practice of contemplation we study the scriptures—the revelations of the seers—with an intention to awaken our dormant inner knowing. In this chapter we examine the nature of consciousness. Study of the nature of consciousness rests on the spiritual practice of self-inquiry. Reading or hearing the teaching, one is directed to inwardly reflect and to inquire deeply. The truth about life is revealed through the light of Supreme Consciousness shining within.

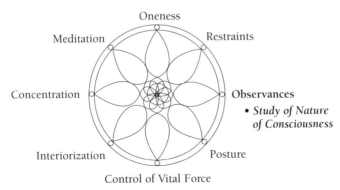

Oneness
Meditation   Restraints
Concentration   Observances
                           • *Study of Nature*
                             of Consciousness
Interiorization   Posture
Control of Vital Force

A Map of Consciousness

The teachings of yoga provide a "map of consciousness" for the seeker. This "map" is the careful rendering of the terrain of our very existence. Direct exploration in consciousness by the ancient Vedic seers charted this territory of existence.

The Vedic map of consciousness indicates that Supreme Consciousness (Absolute Reality) manifests as the world process. What we see and know and experience in the world of matter is an expression of Supreme Consciousness. It is through divine manifestation that all of life exists.

Certain principles form the foundations for this theory of world manifestation. They are:

It is through Divine Manifestation that all of life exists.

1. Supreme Consciousness is the ultimate Reality.

2. This one true Reality is the cause and substance of all manifestation.

3. The Godhead is the first manifestation of Supreme Consciousness.

4. There are three qualities inherent to the Godhead.

For the sake of understanding the complex interconnection of Spirit and matter, the nature of reality is discussed as having various components:

- Supreme Consciousness or Spirit

- Godhead

- Soul

- Mind

- Emotion

- Physical body

As has been noted, all is Supreme Consciousness. Therefore, nothing has separate existence. No part—God, the soul, or the physical body—exists in and of itself alone. All are rooted in Supreme Consciousness, and therefore interrelated.

We have some sense of this in our own experience and in the discoveries of modern science. Where does the life of the body begin and end? Can the physical body maintain existence without the essential support of the soul? Where does the soul end and the body begin? Where is the dividing line between body and mind or spirit and matter?

God, soul, and the physical body...are all rooted in Supreme Consciousness.

Of course, we find we cannot make these distinctions. The boundaries between components of our existence blur because they are truly not separate and distinct. We exist as an energetic continuum. Yet it is possible to examine and discover certain characteristics of the various aspects of the Self.

Nature of Spirit

Supreme Consciousness is the one Reality: That which is. Supreme Consciousness exists both in and beyond the world process. It is the essential Truth of all that exists, yet remains untouched or unmoved by any aspect of creation.

An ancient Vedic hymn describes the transcendental Reality of Supreme Consciousness:

> I salute the Supreme Teacher, the Truth, whose nature is bliss, who is the giver of the highest happiness, who is pure wisdom, who is beyond all qualities and infinite like the sky, who is beyond words, who is one and eternal, pure and still, who is beyond all change and phenomena and who is the silent witness to all our thoughts and emotions—I salute Truth, the Supreme Teacher.

The *Bhagavad Gita* states in chapter seven:

> Those who are not spiritually awake imagine Consciousness as being in creation only. They are unaware of the higher nature which is beyond creation—pure, unseen, and changeless. The truth about Supreme Consciousness—that It remains ever eternal, unborn, and unchanging—is veiled by the creative power of maya (illusion) and not revealed to the unawakened.

Consciousness...is changeless and beyond manifestation.
—Bhagavad Gita

Spirit, or Supreme Consciousness which exists as the one true Reality, is the cause and substance of the process of creation from the subtle to the gross realms. The *Bhagavad Gita* teaches the following:

> Earth, water, fire, air, ether, mind, understanding, and self-sense—these are the eight divisions of Spirit that make creation possible. This is the lower, or creative nature of Spirit. One can also know the higher nature of Spirit, the Oversoul, which upholds all creation. All beings have their beginning in Spirit. Spirit is the origin of all creation and its dissolution. There is nothing greater than Spirit. All creation is strung on Spirit like rows of gems on a string.

All creation is strung on Spirit as rows of gems on a string.
—Bhavagad Gita

Nature of the Godhead

The Godhead is the first manifestation of Supreme Consciousness as it moves from the transcendental realm toward the creation of the world. Thus Supreme Consciousness has been called the "God" beyond God. Supreme Consciousness is Pure Existence without modifying qualities and exists beyond the Godhead, which has qualities. These qualities allow the creation of the world.

The process of world manifestation is likened to the "breath of God" in which Supreme Consciousness sends forth Its Own Self into the creative process. In cyclical fashion, all creation returns to this Source in time, much like "breathing," in an on-going process of exhalation and inhalation.

Three qualities are inherent to the Godhead, the first outflowing of Supreme Consciousness. They are:

1. Being or Existence (omnipresence)
2. Consciousness (omniscience)
3. Creative Energy or Bliss (omnipotence)

Souls are individualized units of Supreme Consciousness that extend into existence through the creative Source (or God). Because

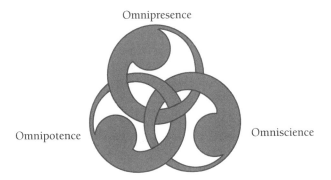

Omnipresence

Omnipotence   Omniscience

the soul is a direct extension of Supreme Consciousness Itself, everyone has the inherent ability to experience this ultimate truth of existence.

The experience of awakening to the truth of existence is the core factor of one's spiritual journey. Liberation of consciousness (freedom from the bondage of false self identification or identification with the ego self) comes through the direct perception of the true Self, or Self-realization. Direct perception is of the soul nature and is beyond thinking mind or mental constructs of any kind.

Through study and direct perception, one comes to understand the deep meaning of the scripture that "we are made in the image and likeness of God" (Supreme Consciousness). It can be discovered that the qualities of the Godhead are inherent to the soul as well.

Because the soul is a direct extension of Supreme Consciousness, everyone has the inherent ability to experience the ultimate Truth of existence.

Nature of the Soul

The soul is defined as an individual, unique aspect of Supreme Consciousness—Divine Essence individualized according to a certain pattern. This pattern is an energetic complex made up of subtle impressions containing the causal elements of both the karmic history of the soul and its purpose for manifesting in a given lifetime.

It is involvement, or attraction, that causes the soul to incarnate, to extend itself into the world. Perhaps this can be thought of as divine curiosity. Whatever the reason, the soul is drawn to incarnate and then through the mind becomes involved with the body and the physical realm. Most often, this involvement is so strong that the true soul identity as Spirit is obscured. This is the spiritual "fall" into forgetfulness of the true nature, from which redemption is necessary.

This error in perception (denial of one's true nature) is said to be the primary cause of suffering. One identified with mind and body assumes the existence of a separate self, or that they are a "body" that has a soul, rather than the truth that one is soul (Spirit individualized) expressing through mind and body.

The following diagrams explore these avenues of perception, that of primarily body/mind identification and that of soul identification.

Perspective of the Spiritually Asleep

This diagram illustrates the "sleep" of ordinary consciousness. It has been so termed by enlightened teachers because when we experience the body/mind/emotion complex as our true identity, we are not spiritually awake but remain asleep to Reality. From this perspective it seems we are primarily a physical body that is operating through emotion, mind, and soul. The perceived influence of God or Spirit is faint, and far away.

From this perspective it is easy to see how one can become preoccupied with the circumstances relating to the body/mind (they seem so all encompassing) and how help or inspiration from Spirit looks unattainable. Holding this viewpoint is considered to be a part of the "human condition."

Georg Feuerstein, in his commentary on the *Yoga Sutra* states:

> Conscious experience is based on a complete reversal of the true relationship between Self and

Spiritually Asleep Perspective

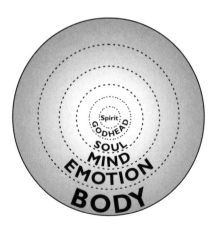

consciousness. Out of nescience [ignorance] the latter arrogates [assigns] to itself the role of subject, thereby lowering the Self to the status of an object. This erroneous reduction of the unchanging, eternal Self to the finite self-consciousness is one of two essential components of human consciousness. The other is the coloration of consciousness by the external objects.

Perspective of the Spiritually Awake

When one is spiritually awake, Spirit is perceived as the Single Reality that is Cause and Support of all that is. Body and mind exist within the realm of Spirit. Here the individual world view is quite different— it is expansive and full of Light. Concerns of the body/mind are tiny in relation to the all-pervasive influence of Spirit.

The arrows indicate that the uplifting, enlightening influence of Spirit flows from the Pure Realm of Spirit all the way to the physical realm of the body. Spirit, God, and soul (expressions of the same Reality) influence the realms of mind and body for healing and regeneration. This path of influence does not occur in reverse. That is, the changes in the body/mind do not affect the integrity of soul, God, or Spirit.

Spirit contains and influences all of life, all beings...but remains forever untouched by them.

Spiritually Awake Perspective

In the *Bhagavad Gita* (chapter nine), we find this stated as the words of the Lord to the seeking soul:

> "I am present throughout the entire universe in My unmanifest form. All beings dwell in Me but I do not dwell in them."

Spirit contains and influences all of life, all beings. It is the source of all manifestation and phenomena but at the same time remains forever untouched by them. So it is that the soul itself retains its pure essence and is ultimately untouched by the patterns and changes of the mind and body. The "redemption" needed from the "fall" is the process of remembering that which has been forgotten. It is spiritual awakening to one's true Self. It does not change the essential nature of the soul which is already spiritual.

When the changing circumstances in the body/mind no longer obscure awareness, the essential nature of the soul is revealed. This is stated in the opening verses of the *Yoga Sutra*:

1. Now begins the way of Yoga (Self-realization).
2. Yoga (Self-realization) is experienced when the fluctuations of the mind cease to obscure Pure Awareness.
3. The soul then dwells in Pure Consciousness, its own essence (Self).
4. When not dwelling in the Self, the soul seems to identify with the mind and its fluctuations.

Because the soul is an individualization of Supreme Consciousness, the qualities of God or the true Self can be discerned and experienced as part of one's own nature. Just as a single drop of ocean water contains the qualities of the great body of water from which it came, so does the soul reflect the divine qualities of its Source. These divine qualities of existence, consciousness, and bliss or creative energy are experienced by the soul in the following ways:

1. Through the quality of existence, one discovers their own nature to be changeless, birthless,

deathless Being—the Absolute Truth that is not subject to change.

2. Through the quality of consciousness, one can know and have awareness.

3. Through the quality of creative energy, one can exercise will, action, creative ability, and experience true joy.

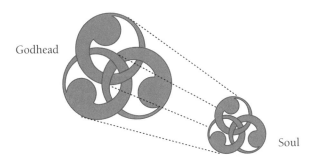

Godhead

Soul

The powers and abilities inherent to God are accessible to the soul.

Nature of Mind and Emotion

Mind

Mind is the subtle medium through which perception is cognized. The totality of mind contains these aspects:

- Conscious

- Subconscious

- Unconscious

- Superconscious

Within the mental field are two components: intelligence (intuition or wisdom) referred to as "buddhi," and thinking mind.

When an individual cognizes through the intelligence or wisdom aspect of mind, the true Self can be discerned and ultimately experienced. This experience of the Self is beyond thought and the thinking mind. When an individual cognizes through the thinking principle, this stimulates feeling and ultimately ego consciousness or

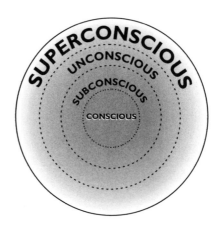

Through the intuitive ability of buddi, we have the ability to "know by knowing," beyond logical analysis.

the sense of separate existence. Through buddhi one is focused on inner reality. Through the ego aspect of mind, one is able to function in and relate to the outer world.

It is through buddi, or awakened intelligence, that one perceives spiritual Truth. However, this aspect of mind is the not Truth itself, but only a "container" of sorts. The seeming sentience of mind is in reality due only to the presence of Spirit.

In Shankara's treatise on Self-knowledge he states:

> "The mind and the sense-organs are illumined by Atman (Supreme Consciousness) alone, as a jar or pot is illumined by a lamp. These material objects cannot illumine their own Self."

Mind, as a subtle medium, not only facilitates perception, but acts as a sort of "storehouse" of impressions made on the mental field. These impressions, particularly those combined with feeling, are the material of "karma," that which will later influence choices. The impressions in the mental field are like seeds which will ripen in time, given the right environment and conditions. Through the practice of Superconscious meditation and self-discipline, one may clear impressions from the mental field. Thus, it is possible to disrupt the karmic, reactive cycle of influence and attain true freedom.

Emotion

While emotion and mind are intimately connected, it is possible to discern emotion as an energetic experience arising within and moving through the body/mind. The realms of influence of thought and feeling interpenetrate. While certain thoughts may give rise to associated feelings, it is also true that certain feelings can give rise to a particular thought cluster.

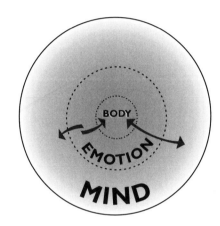

From the spiritual perspective, awareness of thoughts and feelings can contribute to one's growth and awakening. One may discover, through "following" certain thoughts or feelings with one's witness consciousness, the depth impressions stored in the mental field. Inquiry, from the perspective of soul awareness (awakened consciousness), can lead one to recognize and consciously release impressions in the mental field which are not in harmony with one's soul.

While thoughts and feelings may be consciously investigated and can assist in the process of self-discovery, the ultimate experience of the truth of existence transcends mind and emotion. The body, mind, senses, and ego are all subject to modification and thus are "unreliable" vehicles for perceiving that which is beyond modification.

The ultimate experience of the Truth of existence transcends mind and emotion.

The spiritual practices of meditation, self-discipline, and inquiry are tools to help the seeker cross the turbulent waters of the thinking mind and find true peace in the stillness of the Self.

Nature of the Body

The body is the temple of the Holy Spirit.

The body is rightly called the temple of the Holy Spirit or the house of the soul. It is the sacred dwelling place in which Divine Essence resides and through which divine purpose is carried out. Those who are spiritually ignorant see the body as purely physical, a mechanical, biological organism. When seen through this lens, the body is reduced to being a material object and its sacred function is ignored. With spiritual awakening, one comes to respect and honor the body's direct relationship with the Divine.

The physical body is like a garment that the soul wears in any given lifetime. This is no ordinary garment, however. It is a magical garment! It is "magical" in that it is full of surprises, it carries with it records of mystery, and is capable of transformation.

The "magic" or power of the body, of course, originates from the soul. When the soul force, or Spirit power, is removed from the physical body, it has no life of its own.

> Just as the unchanging soul passes in one body through the changes of childhood, youth and age, so is its taking on of another body. As a person discards worn-out garments and puts on others that are new, so does the soul discard worn-out bodies and embody others that are new.
>
> —*Bhagavad Gita*, Chapter II

The physical body we experience as our vehicle for expression in this lifetime is the material manifestation of elements having their origins in subtle coverings of the soul. There exist in the subtle realms various levels of unfolding from the light subtle bodies to the dense material body vehicle.

Coverings of the Soul

The coverings of the soul are referred to as sheaths. The sheaths are progressive in their inclination toward the density of matter required for physical manifestation. The five sheaths represent five levels of consciousness on the soul's journey into the physical plane. They are:

the bliss sheath, the intelligence sheath, the mind sheath, the vital force (breath) sheath, and the physical (food) sheath. The light coverings of the soul act as "blueprints" for the physical body.

The sheaths join together to make up three "bodies" and provide the connecting links to the five levels of consciousness. The three bodies represent the physical, mental, and spiritual dimensions of our being. Without spiritual awakening people are only aware of the physical plane and the physical body; as intuitive abilities unfold one becomes aware of the astral and causal bodies as well. The characteristics of each body are as follows:

The physical body:

- formed by the food and breath sheaths
- associated with the waking state of consciousness
- connects with the astral body through the vital force sheath (breath)
- has a material form
- dimension: physical

Characteristics of the physical body

The astral body:

- formed by the vital force sheath (breath), mind sheath, and intelligence sheath
- associated with the dream state
- connected with the causal body through the intelligence sheath
- has a subtle form similar to the physical body
- dimension: mental

Characteristics of the astral body

The causal body:

- formed by the intelligence sheath and the bliss sheath
- associated with the deep sleep state

Characteristics of the causal body

63

- carries the karmic blueprint of the soul

- connects with soul/Spirit through the bliss sheath

- is an egg-shaped body of light

- dimension: spiritual

The causal body is "closest" to the soul and links directly to the true Self through bliss, one of the three qualities of Spirit shared with the soul nature. The other two qualities of Spirit—consciousness and existence—are transcendent and thus independent of any material manifestation. The causal body carries within it the karmic patterns that endure through various lifetimes. As the karmic patterns stored in the causal body change, the astral and physical bodies change. New astral and physical bodies are formed with each incarnation, while the causal covering of the soul remains. When the soul is liberated, freed from bondage to any residual impressions, the causal body merges back into the Self, its conscious origin.

Energy as a Vehicle for Awakening

The spiritual energy, or life force, that supports the various bodies is a connecting factor that runs through them all from the Source. Thus awareness of energy is a vehicle for awakening, allowing access to the various levels of being from the physical through the subtle to the spiritual. Energy allows communication and integration of the various aspects of one's total being. It is possible, through the vehicle of energy, to bring into harmony soul, mind, and body.

There are many modalities for working with energy in this way. Maps of how subtle energy flows through the body exist in both the science of yoga as the chakra system and in Chinese medicine as the energy meridians.

Spiritual energy pervades all levels of being.

The chakras are centers of energy in the astral body that provide the energetic pathways for vital force from the soul level to flow into the body/mind. The word "chakra" means wheel, which refers to the round shape and spinning movement of these energy vortexes. The chakras, as other aspects of the subtle body, were revealed to ancient seers through introspection. As aspects of our own subtle body, the characteristics of the chakras may be discerned in deep contemplation. In section three of the *Yoga Sutra*, Patanjali refers to the soul powers that arise from perfect contemplation of the chakra centers.

The chakra system notes seven main subtle centers, which correspond with areas of the physical body in the following way:

Chakra	Physical Body Correspondence
Muladhara	Sacrococcygeal plexus (root) at the base of the spine
Swadhishthana	Prostatic plexus
Manipura	Solar plexus
Anahata	Cardiac plexus. Heart center at the middle of the chest
Vishuddha	Laryngeal plexus at the throat
Ajna	Cavernous plexus at the third eye or middle of the forehead
Sahasrara	"Crown" at the top of the head connects with the pineal gland

Vital force flows from the Source into the subtle body through the chakras and into the physical body through the nervous system and nerve branches.

Each chakra corresponds to a level of consciousness with the progression from the root to the crown revealing the soul's journey of awakening from identification with matter to ultimate freedom in the true Self. The first three chakras—the root, the lumbar, and the solar plexus—are significant to building a foundation for being in the world and relate to psychological issues such as security, sexuality, success, and self-esteem. Here one also builds a foundation for a healthy spiritual life through trusting the Universe and learning to work with the subtle energies of the mind and consciousness to achieve success. The heart is the door to the inner realms, a pivotal center, where one enters the way of surrender and discipleship desiring only to follow the divine plan and to live according to Its purpose. The transition leads to the more subtle perceptions of divine truth revealed in the throat, third eye, and crown chakras. When the flow of vital force is stabilized at the crown chakra one attains samadhi, or oneness with the divine Self.

As we explore the truth of who we are through the practice of contemplation, we can find stability and security in an ever-changing world. Outer conditions continually change; inner thoughts and feelings arise and pass away, while the soul nature, the true Self, remains ever serene.

Identifying with this unchanging aspect of the Self is the basis of the spiritual exercise of affirmation. In the face of challenging conditions, one can honestly affirm, "I am ever peaceful and serene." Or, in time of seeming limitation, "I am infinitely abundant." These affirmations are not intended to deny the existence of present conditions but to raise one's consciousness to a higher level of understanding. Yes, challenge and limitation do exist. However, they have no independent existence and they are in a continual process of change. Only the divine Self is unchanging and stable. When we affirm, we look through the challenge, realize it will change, and know the higher true Self to be the basis of our prosperity. Instead of identifying with changing outer circumstances, we rely on our connection to the Source of all. As we raise our consciousness through the use of affirmation we align ourselves—physically, mentally, emotionally, and spiritually—with the power to change our lives for the good. This new alignment reveals itself as healing and as opportunities previously unseen.

And you shall know the truth, and the truth shall make you free.
—John 8:32

PREPARING THE WAY

The tendency of the mind is to separate, divide, and limit, where the essence of Spirit is beyond limitation. Affirmation can be a useful tool to direct the mind toward divine remembrance.

1. Write an affirmation to expand your awareness of who you are. Sample affirmations: I am Truth. I am infinitely creative. I am Peace.

   Your own affirmation:

   Recall your affirmation throughout the day and notice if you have any changes in attitude or perception.

2. Explore some basic avenues of self care.

   What nurtures the soul?

   What nurtures the mind and emotional nature?

   What nurtures the body?

   Caring for all aspects of our being is essential to our health. Take some time this week to actively nurture each aspect of your Self.

3. Can you recall a significant dream where you experienced the astral body? Write about the dream and your own perception of the astral world that is accessible through the dream state.

WORLD PROCESS

> The world is a rotating wheel…All things have one
> root. There are transcendental beings such as angels,
> which have no connection to the material. There is
> the celestial world, whose essence is very tenuous.
> Finally, there is the world below, which is
> completely physical. All three come from different
> realms, but all have the same root.
>
> —Rabbi Nachman

For the Supreme One to become (what appears to be) "many," to manifest as the worlds, there is first an "urge" or an inclination toward creation. Why does Pure Spirit, which is Self-contained and Self-fulfilled, move into manifestation and create the worlds? Sages throughout time have answered: because It does. There is no logical answer to this question, no rational way to discern "why."

Creation myths of the great religions attempt to address this question and to identify the archetypal patterns of life in the cosmos. Some say the worlds were created for the sake of experience. Some say they were created for delight. All seem to agree that the worlds exist for the sake of Spirit. For the soul, the worlds exist as a way to experience, containing the potential for spiritual awakening. With spiritual awareness, one knows the world and all that happens in it to be for the purpose of awakening to the Divine.

With spiritual awareness, one knows the world and all that happens in it to be for the sake of awakening to the Divine.

In our world today, it is possible to see the need for spiritual awakening on a mass scale. How would our world be different if all people were spiritually awake and knew the world to be sacred? How would our life on earth be transformed by the vision of Oneness? What could life be like if people were aware that their purpose in life is to awaken to the divine Self and that the world is the sacred vehicle for this awakening process?

The worlds are said to flow out of Spirit much like a spider makes its web out of its own body. The world is the body of God. This world body, though part of God, contains only a fraction of the allness of Spirit. The creation of the world arises out of the realm of Pure Existence when qualities are introduced into the field of consciousness.

These qualities mix with one another, becoming the primary "ingredients" of creation.

Sacred Vibration

As Supreme Consciousness moves into manifestation, an energetic vibration occurs between the poles of the outflowing force of Creative Energy and the returning (or attracting) force of Consciousness. This vibration has been identified as the sacred Word—known variously in different religious faiths as Om, Amen, Aum, Pranava, and the Nada Brahma. As this sound vibration moves in the direction of manifestation, the qualities of time, space, motion, and atoms appear and make creation possible.

In the beginning was the Word…

In the *Yoga Sutra*, it is stated in chapter one:

> "The manifesting symbol of God is the syllable Om (Word Aum). By reciting the Word and meditating on it, one contemplates its true meaning. By meditation on Om, one realizes the Self—all distractions and obstacles are removed."

In the New Testament, John 1:1-5, one finds a similar teaching:

> "In the beginning was the Word, and the Word was with God. The same was in the beginning with God. All things were made by God; and without God was not anything made that was made. In God was life; and the life was the light of all people. And the light shineth in the darkness; and the darkness comprehended it not."

This process of world manifestation is one that Vedic seers determine occurs over billions of years. The creation of the worlds is balanced also by a time of dissolution (returning to the Pure Realm) which is without manifestation. The creation and dissolution of the worlds has been called the "breath of God" with its periods of out breathing (creation) and in breathing (dissolution) and the pause in between the breaths (stillness).

As an age ends, all creatures return into My nature,
Arjuna; and I create them again as a new age begins.

—*Bhagavad Gita*

Seven Planes of Existence

According to Vedic cosmology, the worlds are said to contain seven planes or levels of existence. Human beings are usually concerned with the physical plane and generally remain unaware of the existence of any other planes.

As Spirit flows into matter in the creation of the worlds, varying densities of consciousness result, from the lightest, purest realm of Spirit to the most dense, the realm of matter. Because the soul is one with Pure Spirit, it is possible to be aware of the light realms. It is only when, through mind, the soul becomes "bound" to matter (through seeming identification) that one is unaware of the inner, more subtle realms of existence.

The seven planes of existence are:

1. The material realm—the physical level

2. The realm of vital force—breath, or prana

3. The realm of mind (thinking principle) and emotion

4. The realm of intelligence

5. The realm of bliss (Ananda)

6. Pure Consciousness (Chit)

7. Pure Existence or Being (Sat)

As is the microcosm, so is the macrocosm.
—the Upanishads

Each of the first five planes represents a realm of existence and a level of consciousness. This system of cosmology contains the macrocosm and the microcosm. These levels of consciousness exist within the individual and each also represents a realm of existence within the divine universe.

Pure Consciousness and Pure Existence are transcendent aspects of Spirit. Therefore, for these two aspects, there are no realms.

Truth of the Nature of Existence

It is only through spiritual awakening (sometimes referred to as rebirth in Spirit or being "born again") that one is able to discern the subtle truth of the nature of existence. Without spiritual discernment people are caught up in the material or manifest realm only. They identify with what they can perceive through the senses and the thinking mind.

Maya masks or covers the truth of the invisible reality of Spirit.

The mixture of the Word (sound current), time, space, and atoms is called "maya," darkness, or illusion because it masks the truth of the invisible reality of Spirit. Those unable to discern the spiritual Reality in and through all creation are said to be caught in the darkness or delusion of maya. In this condition of darkness, one believes creation is separate from the Source.

The physical realm is only a small fragment of the vast expanse of creation as it flows from the Godhead. The majority of creation exists in the "heavenly" realms: the astral and causal spheres. These spheres are where the subtle "blueprint" for the physical world originates.

Three Natural Tendencies

Throughout creation there are three natural tendencies which appear and interact. These tendencies or qualities, called gunas, have the following characteristics:

1. Positive or uplifting tendency toward clarity, light, or awakening—Sattva or Sattvic

2. Neutralizing or active tendency toward restlessness—Rajas or Rajasic

3. Negative or downflowing tendency toward confusion, heaviness, or inertia— Tamas or Tamasic

These three qualities interact and make up the fabric of nature. Everything that is created is made up of varying combinations of these three tendencies. The qualities interact, move, and change, all within the field of Consciousness which is the only true Reality. Those things we may consider "real" and solid are, in fact, only a combination of changing qualities. Objects have no inherent reality of their own, but are a matrix of energies.

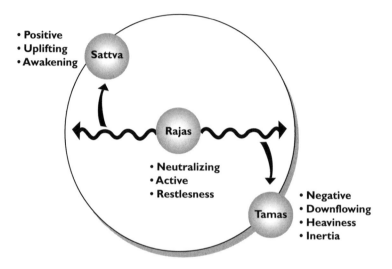

These three qualities in all existence provide a path for discerning one's way toward the light. That is, one can discern, through identifying the characteristics of lightness, restlessness, or inertia, which tendency predominates in any given thing. The devotee will naturally cultivate that which is "sattvic" or has an uplifting influence on consciousness.

The devotee will naturally cultivate that which is sattvic.

The *Bhagavad Gita* states:

> "The three tendencies of nature—uplifting, activating, and dulling—bind the soul to the body. Of these three tendencies, the uplifting tendency encourages health and awakening of consciousness. It also binds the soul to the body through attachment to happiness, knowledge, and noble desires. The activating tendency binds the soul through attachment to action, sense-gratification, and craving. The dulling tendency binds the soul by its inclination toward excess sleep, laziness, and negligence."

These tendencies are found throughout all of nature. Thus, we can learn to identify these tendencies and align our thoughts and actions with the sattvic or uplifting influence, steering away from that which is unsettling (rajasic) or leads to confusion, depression, and despair (tamasic).

A basic example of these tendencies found in nature can be shown through various food choices. Foods containing life force which are close to their natural state are generally sattvic or uplifting, such as an apple. Foods which are heavily spiced are usually rajasic and promote restlessness in the body/mind. Foods which are tamasic or deadening in nature are foods without much nutritional value, foods that are stale or heavily processed which actually tax or harm the body/mind.

Stand by the roads, and look, and ask for the ancient paths, where the good way is; and walk in it.
—Jeremiah 6:16

Positive or Sattvic Environment

One who is serious about spiritual awakening will seek out environments that are sattvic, or uplifting. Such an environment is conducive to awakening and does not impede the natural illumination of the body and mind through the soul. The uplifting influence can be cultivated in all areas of one's life—the choice of physical environment, relationships with people, choices of food and activity, what we choose to focus our attention on, what we read, or watch, or listen to. All of these environmental factors can either contribute to awakening or impede the process.

While it is true that everything exists in Spirit, and therefore anything can be useful to one's awakening, it is advisable to cultivate a positive environmental influence. Environment has a strong impact upon the mind. Especially in the initial stages of awakening, when one has not yet built a solid foundation, it is too easy to be distracted and lose sight of one's spiritual purpose.

We can learn to identify the influences within ourselves and in our present environment. The tendencies within our own body/mind can be used to assist us to move forward toward our goal of spiritual realization. When one is overcome with inertia, laziness, and lack of the will to useful action, the rajasic tendency can be called up. Thus the tendency toward activity which the rajas guna entails can enliven the tamasic tendency toward useful activity. When the rajasic tendency predominates and restlessness is experienced, the sattvic tendency is encouraged to bring balance, peace, and calm to the activating principle.

This side of full awakening, we turn toward the "light," toward that which is uplifting and moves us in the direction of inner calm and greater awakening. The positive quality of sattva, although initially useful for awakening, is still a form of bondage for the soul. As Spirit is beyond all qualities, pure and still, we will ultimately let go of cultivating even the sattvic tendency.

Love—The Attracting Current in World Manifestation

In the process of world manifestation, there is one current or energy that flows out from the transcendental realm into creation, and one which pulls all creation back to Itself. The current that moves into the world is called the Creative or Manifesting Current. The current that brings creation "back" to its Source to return to the field of Pure Consciousness is known as the Attracting Current, also called Love.

"God as Love" refers to That which creates the worlds out of Itself...and calls them back into Its own Being.

When God is referred to as Love, it is the primary essence of existence that is referred to. 'God as Love' means That which creates the worlds out of Itself, and redeems them, calls them back into Its own Being. This Love is not love as an emotion, but Love as existence. We understand that love as emotion is subject to change. God as Love is unchanging, ever constant.

When we define God as Love, we are referring to Love in the highest sense as ever conscious, ever compassionate, and unconditional. Truly as God is Love, the very essence of life, we are never without this divine support.

We have the ability to cultivate divine love in our thoughts, words, and actions. This cultivation of divine love can be a path "home," back to the true Self.

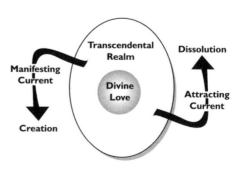

✎ Preparing the Way

1. Begin to identify the tendencies in nature—sattvic, rajasic, and tamasic—that you see manifesting in your environment and the lifestyle choices you are making.

   Consider the various components of your environment. Which of the three tendencies is predominant? Note in the following table.

THE THREE TENDENCIES			
	Sattva Positive, uplifting; tendency toward awakening	Rajas Neutralizing or active; tendency toward restlessness	Tamas Negative or downflowing; tendency toward confusion or heaviness
Books			
Movies & Television			
Work			
Food			
Relationships			
Activities			
Music			
Physical Environment			
Other			

Review the table and think about what would bring more sattvic influence in those areas that are more rajasic or tamasic. Write what those changes would be in the sattvic column.

2. Draw or sculpt an image that represents the world process to you.

How do you see the relationship between Spirit, God, the created worlds, and the individual soul?

How does your view of the cosmos affect your spiritual life?

As is the human body,

so is the cosmic body.

As is the human mind,

so is the cosmic mind.

As is the microcosm,

so is the macrocosm.

As is the atom,

so is the universe.

　　　—The Upanishads

As a candle flame
in a windless place
does not waver,
of such is the likeness
of the meditator's mind.
—*Bhagavad Gita*

Six
Meditation and Prayer

Most of us think compulsively all the time; we talk to ourselves. If I talk all the time I don't hear what anyone else has to say. In exactly the same way, if I think all the time, that is to say if I talk to myself all the time, I don't have anything to think about except thoughts. Therefore, I'm living entirely in the world of symbols and I'm never in relationship with reality. I want to get in touch with reality: that's the basic reason for meditation.

—Alan Watts, *Meditation*

The next section of the Fourfold Practice to be explored is Meditation and Prayer. Meditation is central to Kriya Yoga and encompasses several "limbs" of the eight limbs of practice: Posture, Control of Vital Force, Interiorization, Concentration, and Meditation. Each of the practice limbs preceding true meditation assists in building a firm foundation for the meditative experience. With the cultivation of the virtues, the restraints and observances, one puts an ethical foundation in place. The ethical foundation allows one to turn their attention inward without undue distraction from a life out of balance. The

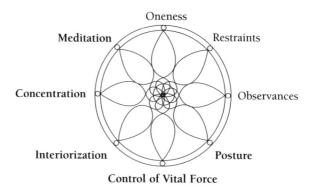

limbs that follow address the progressive process of turning attention within through the stages that culminate in meditative absorption.

THE PRACTICE OF MEDITATION

Meditation practice is the foundation for being able to access states of consciousness usually beyond our ordinary perception. In our normal waking consciousness, thought activity fills the mental field, absorbs our attention, and obscures our awareness of the silent true Self. Through the practice of meditation, thought activity subsides, the mental field clears, and one experiences the non-ordinary perception of the still silence of Being. While this experience is natural to human beings and many people experience it spontaneously—as clarity, as a spiritual experience, or as a heightened state of awareness—a practice such as meditation is necessary to be able to access it at will.

Meditation is resting in the Self, experiencing the pure silence of the soul nature without thought activity. During meditation, attention flows continuously to the pure aspect of one's being. Meditation can also be described as preparing the inner environment so that one may experience this clear aspect of their own being. As a spiritual discipline, meditation is an exercise practiced in many different forms, most of which attempt to provide access to one's innermost clarity.

Meditation is continual dwelling in Divine Consciousness

In the highest sense, meditation is continual dwelling in Divine Consciousness, a way of being continually aware of one's true existence as the imperishable divine Self. The exercises of meditation practice are preparation for being able to access at will this altered state of non-ordinary consciousness.

In the heart
is a well, filled
with the sound of silence.
Drink

from it.
One taste
changes everything.

How do I know?
The day I stopped

sitting on the edge
and fell in,
told me this.
—Ellen Grace O'Brian,
The Sanctuary of Belonging

What Happens During Meditation

- The physical body relaxes and stress is released from the system.

- The meditator becomes less attached to and identified with the contents of the body/mind and instead becomes the "conscious witness" (soul identification).

- There is a withdrawal from sense perception and from involvement with the objects of the senses. The mental field becomes clear.

- Internal states become more vivid and attractive.

- The urge for outer experience becomes neutralized.

- As identification with contents of the mind is released, one experiences peace and inner freedom.

- One experiences the true Self, or the clear aspect of Being.

- Following the "peak experience" of clarity for that occasion, one returns attention fully to mind and body awareness.

Preparation for Meditation

Posture

Meditation begins with attention to posture (asana)—both the position of the physical body and one's attitude of mind. Physical posture must be comfortable and relaxed, yet alert. Meditation, although a calm experience, is not passive—it is active. It is active in the sense that one's focus and attention are intentionally brought forth to allow one to experience an altered state of consciousness. One's physical posture should reflect the inner intentionality of the process.

One's physical posture should reflect the inner intentionality of the meditation process.

An upright position is recommended for sitting meditation whether on a chair or the floor. Lying down (especially for newcomers to meditation) is not recommended. Since we are conditioned to fall asleep in the lying down posture, it is not considered conducive to the alertness or intentionality necessary for meditation.

The sitting position should be comfortable and relaxed, with attention given to the spinal column being straight. Subtle vital force flows into the body/mind through the spinal pathway. Keeping the spine and head erect allows this vital force to flow easily upward. The upward flow of vital force contributes to concentration and to being able to remain alert and awake. If the head is allowed to bend down toward the body, the energy tends to flow down into the body, bringing one's attention with it. It is more difficult to maintain the position of witness (conscious observer of phenomena) if one is identified with the body.

The initial discipline of meditation is simply learning to sit. It is important to learn the discipline of how to remain unmoving—first with the body, and then the mind. Therefore it is helpful to find a comfortable pose where one will not continually be drawn to adjusting the body position.

Sitting is preparation for the more subtle work with the mind.

As one begins the practice of sitting with the intention of keeping one's seat, or remaining still for a period of time, there will be an opportunity to observe inclinations toward restlessness, urges to move the body that will come and go. This is preparation for the more subtle work with the mind where one sits with pure awareness, watching the thoughts and feelings arise and pass away while remaining uninvolved.

Control of Vital Force

Vital force is the subtle energy of consciousness that brings awareness and life to our being. In our normal waking conscious state, vital force is animating the body/mind and generally flows out through the senses into involvement with the outer world. This is because the energy of our awareness is usually directed outward, attaching itself to the objects of the senses.

In the practice of meditation the outflow of vital force is reversed and attention is consciously withdrawn from the senses and outer involvement. In yoga science this control of vital force is called pranayama. There are specific exercises, such as alternate nostril breathing, that are designed to support the regulation and control of vital force. Some conditions resulting from yogic practices that would be considered miracles to normal thinking are manifestations of the control of vital force. Such occurrences would include the ability to slow one's heart rate, lower one's blood pressure, or remain conscious for extended periods of time without food or breathing.

Interiorization

Interiorization is the neutralization of the outward flow of vital force or attention known in yoga practice as pratyahara. When this stage is established, one's attention is more strongly anchored in inner perception than in outer. In our ordinary waking consciousness, we remain largely externalized with our attention, more aware of what is outside of the body/mind than we are aware of the more subtle inner states and perceptions.

We are drawn progressively inward, to more subtle experience and awareness.

When, through the reversal of the flow of vital force, interiorization occurs, inner reality holds a stronger fascination than outer perception. We are drawn progressively inward, to more subtle experience and awareness.

Concentration

Concentration, or dharana, occurs when attention is steady at one point and remains unwavering. With one-pointed attention comes the stilling of thought activity as the mind holds steady. With this steadiness of mind and attention, the natural clarity of soul perception becomes available. The clear awareness of the true Self is ever present but is usually obscured by the continual fluctuations of the mind. When the mind is steady, through concentration, what is generally "background" to our awareness becomes foremost in our awareness.

Although concentration at first necessitates an act of will (the control of vital force), it is the natural outcome of interiorization and is therefore essentially effortless. Concentration is not a forcing of attention but a flowing of attention. Posture, control of vital force, interiorization, and concentration naturally and effortlessly evolve into meditation. Samadhi, or the experience of Oneness, occurs through divine grace in the natural progression of the opening provided by meditation.

There are two major types of meditation:

1. Concentration meditation involves the directing of attention to a single focus such as a mantra, the experience of the breath, or an image.

2. Mindfulness meditation emphasizes detached observation of what arises in the mind from one moment to the next, rather than restricting awareness to one object of attention.

Concentration Meditation

Concentration meditation practice provides a useful foundation for mindfulness practice and other spiritual disciplines as well. Learning to direct and focus attention is a skill that has far-reaching benefits in all areas of one's life.

Experience calming of the fluctuations in the mental field through concentration.

In concentration practice, one develops pure concentration on a single focus and experiences a calming of the fluctuations in the mental field. When attention wanders or is distracted by other stimuli, the attention is simply returned to the chosen point of focus.

Thoughts, feelings, or sensations that arise are released when the attention is returned to the chosen focus. Such occurrences are treated as distractions to one's point of focus and thus are not followed or investigated.

With the practice of steady, one-pointed concentration, one's attention becomes progressively interiorized and sensitized to subtle inner perception such as inner sound, light, energy, or peace. These subtle objects of concentration become a focus, an "anchor" for the wandering and unsteady mind. When the mind becomes calm through steady concentration, the peace of the soul begins to permeate the mental field.

Mindfulness Meditation

In mindfulness meditation, the skill of detached observation is grounded by concentrating on one primary object (like the breath) initially to stabilize attention, then allowing the range of attention to expand to ultimately include all that arises in each moment.

The ability to practice detached self-observation develops with consistent practice.

The ability to practice detached self-observation and expand one's awareness in the moment develops with consistent practice. As one practices noticing what arises in the mind and body from the conscious witness perspective, the mind will tend to become attached to the objects that arise. The discipline of mindfulness meditation is to:

- allow the arising,
- notice what is arising,
- allow it to pass through the mind and body
   without attaching the attention to it.

The tendency of the mind to wander, become distracted, and caught up in thought content is a significant obstacle in meditation. When the mind wanders and attaches to content, one experiences a reduction or a complete loss of moment-to-moment attention, awareness, and observation.

When the attention becomes involved with the contents of the mind, and the meditator becomes conscious of it, attention is then returned to a detail of present reality, like the movement of the breath. When the experience of detached observation becomes stable once again, the field of awareness can be expanded. In meditation, the value placed on all thought content, feelings, or sensory experience is the same. All such happenings are simply noted as they arise.

BENEFITS OF MEDITATION PRACTICE

The impression of "I am Supreme Consciousness,"
which comes as a result of uninterrupted reflection,

destroys ignorance and its distractions, as a special
medicine destroys disease.

—Shankara, from *The Atmabodha*,
his treatise on Self-knowledge

Consistent practice of meditation is beneficial on all levels of being—
physical, mental, emotional, and spiritual—and supports our ability
to make positive life changes. The discipline required to maintain a
meditation practice is an investment in spiritual self-care. Some benefits, such as enhanced relaxation, are immediately noticeable while
others that are more subtle are observed only as spiritual awareness
unfolds. With the enhanced awareness that accompanies meditation
practice, life is experienced as a dynamic flow, the harmonious
expression of Divine Love.

Physical

- Meditation relieves stress from the mind and body. Brain waves
  indicate less oxygen is consumed, less carbon dioxide is given off,
  blood lactate levels are reduced, and blood pressure is normalized.

- Improved physical health is encouraged as the individual becomes
  more aware of body signals indicating levels of stress and relaxation.

Mental and Emotional

- One experiences calmness and the peace that is natural to the soul
  nature.

- Powers of concentration are increased.

- Creative abilities are enhanced.

- Meditators increase their ability to overcome habits and dependencies.

*Meditation supports
our ability to make
positive changes.*

Spiritual

- Intuitive abilities are enhanced as intuitive wisdom becomes more
  accessible.

- One can experience the true Self during meditation, that which is
  beyond body or mind identification. This opens the doorway to

Self-realization which then is a dynamic force of transformation in all areas of one's life and all levels of understanding.

Benefits in Daily Life

There is a tendency for people to want great breakthroughs in consciousness and ecstatic meditation experiences as soon as they begin practicing. It is important to remember that the experience of the divine Self comes through divine grace. With any spiritual practice, we are simply clearing the way to encourage perception when it happens. The ecstasies of the saints were built upon a firm foundation of cultivating the virtues as well as the practices of prayer and meditation.

The benefits of meditation are initially observed in one's daily life rather than within the sitting practice itself. Observe yourself over time in your daily life as you practice meditation. Are you becoming a calmer, more peaceful person? Are you able to let go a little easier, and be a little less attached to specific outcomes? Are you more relaxed? Do you notice more frequent flashes of intuition? Are you better able to concentrate or focus your attention?

The successful practice of meditation is encouraged through a steady commitment to practice combined with non-attachment to the results of practice. There will be times of peak experience—inner light, energy perception, sound, or deep clarity and peace. These experiences are to be appreciated and then, let go. If one tries to duplicate an inner experience, the attachment to the outcome will become a barrier.

Appreciate peak experiences and then, let them go.

LEARNING TO MEDITATE

> Look into that closed room, the empty chamber where brightness is born! Fortune and blessing gather where there is stillness. But if you do not keep still—this is what is called sitting but racing around.
>
> —Chuang Tzu

Have a Regular Practice

Make a commitment to a regular, daily meditation schedule and keep it. This is the most significant key to successful practice. Sporadic practice brings minimal results.

The tao of heaven and earth becomes visible through perserverance.
—I Ching

With a regular practice one gains the self-discipline so vitally necessary to the process of turning attention from attachment and identification with the physical to spiritual realization. You will also find that although some degree of will is needed initially to set up a regular practice, as you increasingly experience the higher pleasure of communion with the divine Self, you will find yourself naturally drawn to meditate.

Create a Sacred Space

Create a comfortable and sacred environment for your meditation practice. Have a sacred space in your home where you regularly meditate, reserving a chair or cushion solely for your practice. While an altar is often a part of the formal structure of worship in churches and temples, it is also important to one's spiritual life to "bring the altar home." Traditionally a symbol of sacrifice, the altar represents the place where soul and Spirit meet when the ego is surrendered. You can create an altar with a simple table and items that help you cultivate your devotional nature such as pictures of the saints, candles, incense, or flowers. The daily ritual of tending the altar in your home contributes to your practice being holistic—involving body, mind, heart, and soul nature.

Your sacred space will become charged with the energy of your devotion and meditation and will draw your attention to peace and Divine remembrance. Just as we are conditioned to think of food when passing by the refrigerator, so do we infuse our home with thoughts of God or Goddess through the presence of an altar.

Turn Off (or Down) Interruptions

Schedule your meditation practice for a time when you are not likely to be interrupted, and remove environmental distractions as much as possible—put the cat out, turn off the ringer on the phone, turn off the sound on the answering machine. Let people know you will be unavailable for awhile. This is a foundational practice for being able to detach from reliance on outside stimuli.

Choose the Right Time

Choose a time to meditate when you are not too tired, have not just eaten, are not physically ill or overly stressed. Early in the morning before beginning one's day is a recommended time, before the mind becomes too involved with externals. The natural break periods at noon, at sunset, just before dinner, or at the end of your day are other recommended times. If you meditate twice a day, you will find that one meditation supports the other and that inner calm is more easily accessed.

Gradually Increase the Time

Usually ten minutes spent in meditation at first, then increased to twenty or thirty minutes per session, is useful. A ten minute or even twenty minute meditation is generally just enough time to calm the mind and to begin practice. It is like just a little taste of honey!

Dive deep into the ocean of Divine Consciousness to discover the pearl of realization.

The more one yearns for Divine experience, the more consistent and deep must be the meditation and prayer practice. The beginner in meditation is like a would-be swimmer who stands at the shore getting her feet wet. Those who whole-heartedly pursue meditation dive deep into the ocean of consciousness by devoting extended periods of time and focused energy to their practice. Learn the discipline of consistent sitting, then gradually increase the time spent in the inner realms.

Include Prayer with Meditation

When defined as dwelling in Divine Consciousness, the practice of meditation is a form of prayer. In the preparatory stages of practice, prior to the experience of true meditation, it can be helpful to pray for attunement. Call upon your awareness of the divine Presence, however you conceive It. Acknowledge It all around you and within you. Call upon your awareness of the saints and sages and invite the influence of their consciousness. As there is one Life, Power, and Presence common to us all, we can inwardly commune with the great ones through our connection to the Source.

As we pray for attunement, initially we use the mind and feeling nature to invite soul knowledge to predominate our awareness. This invitation to remember who we are as one with the Divine is later experienced in consciousness as the meditation deepens into knowing, or meditative awareness.

Once we are established in the truth of our divine nature, there is no need to be fulfilled; neither is there a separate Self to make requests of. Prayer has gone beyond the mental realm into the experience of resting in pure Being. During this experience, Superconscious energy influences the body, mind, and emotional nature toward healing. Prayers for help or healing for self or others are best done after meditation when one has touched Divine Presence and feels Its influence.

After experiencing Divine Presence in meditation, one can affirm the truth of this one Power and Presence in all of life that sees to harmony and right action. Thoughts of fear, lack, or limitation are surrendered into the experience of Divine realization.

Instruction for Concentration Meditation

Begin with prayer and attention to posture.

1. Sit with the body relaxed and the spinal column straight. Sitting either on the floor or in a chair is fine, as long as the body is comfortable and you will be able to remain in that position without moving for a time.

   Begin with a prayer of invocation and attunement, calling into your awareness Divine Presence around and within you.

Direct attention inward.

2. Close your eyes and bring your attention to the inflowing and outflowing breath. Gradually withdraw your attention from external involvement and become more internalized with your focus.

Bring attention upward.

3. As the body begins to relax and your attention becomes more interiorized, allow your attention to flow to the subtle energy centers, either the third eye (at the center of the eyebrows) or the crown chakra (just beyond the top of the head).

Focus on a single point.

4. You can anchor your attention at the vital center where you have focused by remaining aware of the breath. To

focus at this single point, you might want to imagine or "feel" that the breath enters and exits the body though this point of concentration.

5. Once the mental field has become calm and concentration is stable, let go of the intense focus on the breath and simply rest in the inner peace that is revealed.

Let go and rest in inner peace.

6. Whenever you notice that you have begun to be involved with thinking again, simply return to your point of focus at the vital center, being aware of the natural flow of your breath.

Bring your focus back if you wander.

7. After experiencing the peak experience for that occasion of meditation, spend some time in prayer, sharing the sense of Divine Influence with all who come into your consciousness.

Pray.

8. Bring your attention slowly back to mind and body involvement. Gently return your attention to the surrounding environment.

Return slowly.

9. Spend a few moments allowing your meditative consciousness to infuse your body/mind, and joyfully anticipate your day or evening ahead.

Be in joy!

Instruction for Mindfulness Meditation

1. Sit in a comfortable and relaxed position, with the spine straight. Take a deep breath, exhale, and let go of any tension you are holding in your body. Close your eyes and with the next breath, feel as if you are pulling your attention within, away from external distractions.

Release tensions and move your attention inward.

2. Bring to mind your awareness of omnipresent Divine Spirit—everywhere around you and within you. Feel your own connection with the Source.

Connect with the Source.

Be aware of each breath.	3. Be mindful (aware) of each breath, noticing the rising and falling movement of the abdomen. Allow the breath to be easy, coming and going at its natural rhythm. Feel the sensations with each breath, noticing what is actually there in the body each moment.
Note distractions by labeling.	4. When distractions from focusing on the breath arise, such as sounds in the environment, make a mental note of "hearing, hearing" while you focus your attention on the actual experience of the sound as opposed to its meaning or content.
Return attention to breathing if you wander.	5. Allow the noting of attention and the mindfulness of the breath to be as continuous as possible. Anytime you notice the mind has wandered into thought, simply note "wandering," and then return your attention to the breathing.
Note sensations in the body.	6. When your awareness is drawn to sensations in the body, focus all of your attention on the sensation itself as an observer. Maintain the witness stance. Notice what the qualities of the sensation are and notice if it changes as you observe it.
Always return to mindfulness of breath.	7. Let your breathing be the central, underlying focus of the meditation, returning to it again and again when other objects of awareness disappear from attention.
Expand witness awareness.	8. Once the mind is calm and steady again let the witness awareness expand to a fuller range of sensation and experience, noting each as it arises.
Pray.	9. Before you conclude your time of meditation, share the essential feeling of peace in consciousness with that which you are drawn to pray about. Be aware of distinguishing that which is subject to change and that which is eternal.

10. When you are ready to conclude your meditation, gently bring your awareness fully to mind, body, and back to your surroundings.

Return gently.

The Way of Meditation

The way of meditation is both a skill and an attitude. As a skill it allows us to see clearly who we are and to live our lives with this clarity. Being authentically who we are, moment to moment, brings forth an attitude of trust, an openness toward life, and an acceptance of ourselves and others. The insights experienced in meditation practice resonate in our daily life, extending into it like ripples across a pond.

From meditation arises wisdom. Without meditation wisdom fades.
—*The Dhammapada*

Just as we observe in meditation the transitory nature of thoughts, feelings, and various mind states, so we begin to observe that the conditions in our life are in a constant state of flux. To see clearly this fleeting nature of conditions and experiences brings freedom from suffering. The way of meditation is to see clearly and to live accordingly. In this seeing there is strength and dignity, out of which compassion, forgiveness, acceptance, and love naturally flow.

Meditation is as natural as our breath. We simply open to it and increase our awareness of what is, without effort. Each day, each moment, each meditation, is unique. We can let go of trying to duplicate our own or another person's experience.

The brilliance of the inner critic or judging mind fades in the light of meditation. The tyrannical nature of the judging mind can be tremendously oppressive when one knows no alternative. Meditation shows us the alternative to buying into this limited notion of self. The honor and respect we afford ourselves through our commitment to daily practice is returned to us in serenity.

Most importantly, meditation affords us the opportunity to know through direct experience who we are as spiritual beings. Knowledge of the true Self is the basis for transforming our personality and our life. Once we realize through our own experience that our nature is birthless, deathless, eternal Being, the fears and anxieties of life in this world fade. The yogi saint Mahavatar Babaji was noted to offer this wisdom as solace to his devotees: even a small amount of superconscious meditation can remove fear. Once fear is quelled, the natural joy inherent to the soul nature becomes apparent.

PREPARING THE WAY

> Prayer is the key of the morning and the bolt
> of the evening.
>
> —Mahatma Gandhi

1. Set a daily meditation schedule and commit to it.

   Mark on your calendar each daily meditation. This will
   assist you in maintaining the schedule. Use the chart below
   for your first week. If you miss any scheduled meditation,
   make up the time before going to bed that night.

	Scheduled Meditation	Length of Meditation	Actual Time and Length of Meditation
Day 1			
Day 2			
Day 3			
Day 4			
Day 5			
Day 6			
Day 7			

   Schedule one day during your week to meditate for an
   extended period of time to expand your ability. Mark that day
   on the chart for your first week.

2. Create and care for your altar and sacred meditation space in
   your home.

3. Participate in a group meditation experience.

The fragrance of sandalwood
does not travel far.
But the fragrance of virtue
Rises to the heavens.

                          —Dhammapada

Seven
Cultivating the Virtues

Without reducing negative qualities, progress in spiritual life is as impossible as carrying water in a sieve.

—Baba Hari Dass

The next section of the Fourfold Practice is self-discipline or Cultivating the Virtues. Self-discipline, as well as being a core element of the Fourfold Practice of Kriya Yoga, also constitutes two of the components of Eight-Limbed Yoga, the restraints and observances.

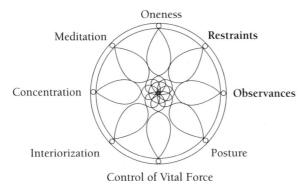

Cultivation of the virtues is central to the practice of self-discipline.

Self-discipline in the deepest sense refers to bringing one's thoughts, words, and actions into alignment with the higher Self. Cultivation of the virtues is central to the practice of self-discipline.

In the initial stages, self-discipline may be concerned with acts of will and behavior modification. Ultimately, true self-discipline is a radical return to the natural integrity of the soul—to doing what one knows to be in alignment with truth. Our conscience, or soul wisdom, lets us know when we err from the path of integrity. When we practice self-discipline we are turning away from thoughts and behaviors that will bring suffering, and we are cultivating thoughts and behaviors that will bring peace and freedom.

When self-discipline through the cultivation of the virtues becomes a spiritual practice, one becomes progressively aware of the subtle aspects of understanding the virtues. With greater understanding, one can move from the surface level of behavior to working with the subtle roots of action such as thoughts, motive, or intention.

Initially, we stop behaving in ways that are not consistent with our spiritual values. Then we explore the underlying causes of the behavior. The next step is the cultivation of the opposite, substituting the virtuous thought and behavior for what previously lacked righteousness.

Self-control and virtuous behavior will not create a spiritual condition; the spiritual condition of pure Being is without cause and is not dependent upon externals such as thoughts or behaviors. The practice of self-discipline is intended to destroy the impurities of thought and behavior that obscure the brightness of the soul—like washing a dusty window pane allows the light to shine through. The value in cultivating the virtues is:

1. clearing the obstructions and chaos that obscure soul wisdom;

2. removing the cause of present and future suffering.

Authentic self-discipline is aligning our thoughts, words, and actions with the intention of the true Self. It is important to keep Self-realization as the focal point of self-discipline, rather than focusing on self-improvement. It is a matter of emphasis. Continual focus on the imperfect small self reveals a never-ending need for improvement, while awareness of needed change with focus on the power of the divine Self allows the transformation to occur. We become aware, willing to change, and then cooperate in the divine process.

KRIYA YOGA

The restraints of Kriya Yoga—harmlessness, truthfulness, non-stealing, right use of vital force, and non-attachment—and the observances—cleanliness, contentment, self-discipline, study of the nature of consciousness, and surrender of the sense of separateness—are consistent with the ethical codes found in all the world's religions. Although both the restraints and observances are pathways to revealing inner wisdom, one could say that the restraints are focused on the self in relationship to others and the world, and the observances are more concerned with the inner life.

Meditation and cultivation of the virtues are inseparable.

All aspects of this spiritual work are interrelated. This is especially true with the practice of meditation and the cultivation of the virtues—they are inseparable. One who does not cultivate the virtues will have difficulty with meditation due to the chaos and unrest in the mental field caused by living a life that does not resonate with the truth. As one cultivates the virtues and brings the outer life into integrity with inner truth, a calming influence of right living pervades the mind and body, making meditation easier. Meditation then facilitates the deeper work with the virtues, making subtle insight more available by allowing access to the inner realms of knowing.

> Birth does not lead to greatness; but the cultivation of numerous virtues leads to greatness.
>
> It is a pearl that possesses real greatness and not the pair of shells in which it is produced.
>
> —Vajjalagam

> Hasten to do even a slight virtue, and flee from transgression; for virtue attracts virtue, and transgression, transgression.
>
> —Judaism, Mishnah

Harmlessness (Ahimsa)

> Ahimsa is not the crude thing it has been made to
> appear. Not to hurt any living thing is no doubt a
> part of ahimsa. But it is its least expression. The
> principle of ahimsa is hurt by every evil thought,
> by undue haste, by lying, by wishing ill to
> anybody. It is also violated by our holding on to
> what the world needs.
>
> —Mahatma Gandhi

Harmlessness can be defined as "non-violence" or "non-harming"—
not causing or wishing harm to oneself or others through thought,
word, or action. Study and practice of harmlessness will reveal that it
goes beyond the passive quality of "not doing" (ceasing from being
harmful) to an active practice of "doing" (being helpful). If we are
truly non-harming, we will be helping.

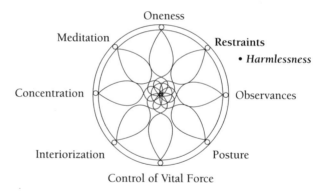

The first stage of harmlessness practice is to stop harming, to
cease behaving in ways that will injure self or others. One can identify behaviors that are violent, that bring injury or death to another
person or animal, and stop those behaviors. There are many behaviors
in our culture which, on the surface, might not appear to be violent
or harmful. Upon deep self-examination and spiritual reflection their
harming tendencies will be revealed. Over-consumption of resources,
having and consuming more than we need, would be one example.

*The first stage of
harmlessness practice
is to stop harming, to
cease behaving in
ways that will injure
self or others.*

Taking the resources of our planet beyond what we individually need contributes to the imbalance of resources that brings about suffering for many in the world who go without basic needs being met. Harmlessness practice assists us in becoming aware of our connection with all of life.

Beyond behavior and actions in the world, harmlessness concerns our words, feelings, and our thoughts. To criticize, to gossip, or think envious thoughts of another is not consistent with harmlessness. One strives to root out violence, such as anger and hatred, from the mental field.

Non-violence is an active force of the highest order. It is soul force or the power of Godhead within us.
—Mahatma Gandhi

Transforming Anger and Hatred

While anger and hatred are natural human reactions, with spiritual discernment one can actually discover the root cause and either transform it or remove it. The root cause of anger is related to thwarted desire, the frustration of not having what one wants. If there is strong identification with the ego structure (the individual "I"), blocked desire will produce anger as a reaction. When one is not so strongly identified with the ego, there is less attachment, and less anger. Where there is attachment, anger can easily follow. Resentment is anger that is held onto and returned to again and again in the mind. Clearing anger and resentments are part of this spiritual practice.

When it comes to letting go of anger and clearing away resentments many people feel "stuck." Here is where discernment, compassion, and forgiveness come in. These qualities help us to release emotion and allow the healing process to move forward.

Discernment

Discernment is our soul ability to see clearly, to know what is true. The ego self needs to be right, so it approaches a situation and tries to establish fault or blame. The soul nature, however, brings forth an openness to higher truth and a willingness to understand the situation holistically.

Through discernment we can discover many things that will help us to let go. We can discover our part in creating a hurtful situation. We can discover the true cause of the harming behavior to be ignorance. People act harmfully when they are not spiritually awake.

Compassion

Experiencing the heart of another's pain with the desire to remove their suffering is compassion. Certain conditions in life have created obstacles to most humans being fully awake. When we recognize that due to their karma, their patterns of conditioning, people act as they do, we can begin to have compassion. People injure others because they themselves are injured, or ignorant.

Forgiveness

Consciousness is the transformative fire where healing occurs.

Forgiveness can happen when we acknowledge the fallibility of humanity (including ourselves) and we turn the resolution of the injury over to the Divine. Sometimes people are resistant to practice compassion or to forgive because they think it means condoning the injurious behavior. It does not. Compassion and forgiveness do not indicate in any way that injurious behavior is acceptable. Just the opposite is true. Compassion and forgiveness are practiced by the spiritually awake so as to not participate in violence or continue the process of harming.

When discernment, compassion, and forgiveness are practiced, then hatred, anger, and the intent to harm are transformed into love by the purifying effects of awakened consciousness. This is the power of Consciousness (Spirit) to heal and transform our lives.

The Foundation for All Other Spiritual Practices

Harmlessness practice is a foundation for all other spiritual practices. The spiritual principle of harmlessness is the awareness that all is God, all is Divine. Therefore, there is no intention to harm anyone or anything in God's sacred creation—not others, not oneself, nor the environment. Taken together, discernment, compassion, and forgiveness reflect the ground of Being, or Divine Love. When we reflect God, we identify with All That Is.

Sometimes people despair that harmlessness practice is simply not possible. They cite the knowledge that just being alive, just walking on the earth, eating, and breathing will cause harm to the environment and bring death to creatures. This tendency to denounce the teaching as unworkable in terms of perfection is based on a lack of understanding.

It is true that our being on the planet in some way will always cause harm. However, harmlessness practice is concerned primarily with consciousness, and secondarily with whatever actions stem from that consciousness. One works on the surface level of behavior to minimize harm to others and the planet but the true work is in removing from one's consciousness all desire to harm.

Yoga is never a "half-way" practice for those who seek full liberation of consciousness. While steps may be taken along the way to prevent harmful behavior as one travels the path of awakening, the ultimate goal for the yogi is to remove all traces of the individual self through many lifetimes of practice, so there is no longer any compulsion driven by desire to return to earth and be an agent of harm in any way.

For most spiritual seekers in the initial stages of awakening, it is sufficient practice to examine what is harmful, to investigate in consciousness why that inclination is present, and to "root it out" or transform it into positive action.

The true work is in removing all desire to harm.

Those who see all creatures within themselves and themselves in all creatures know no fear.
—*Isha Upanishad*

> When one is established in the virtue of harmlessness, all enmity ceases in that person's presence.
>
> —*Yoga Sutra*

In our everyday life, harmlessness practice affects our relationships with others, self, and the earth. The practices of ecological awareness, health and fitness, compassion, and loving kindness are all based in harmlessness. In its most profound sense, harmlessness is related to love. The Buddha said, "Hate never once dispelled hate, only love dispels hate." Only love.

> What sort of spirituality can one have
> without compassion?
> One must show compassion
> to all living beings.
> Compassion is the root
> of all spirituality.
>
> —adapted from *Basavanna*

PREPARING THE WAY

1. Harmlessness and your relationship to yourself.

   Make a commitment to notice and set aside attempts at self-criticism as a spiritual practice. Strive for progress and inner peace, not perfection and outer approval. Write down any understanding you gain about self-criticism.

2. Harmlessness and your relationship to your body.

   Inventory your relationship to your body. Write down some ways that harmlessness practice would help your health and fitness.

3. Harmlessness and your relationship to others.

   Be aware of your thoughts and actions toward others. Focus on positive and helpful speaking and let go of any urge to criticize or gossip. Write down any insights about your relationship to others.

4. Harmlessness and your relationship to the planet.

   Be aware of the choices of your lifestyle. How do these choices affect life on our planet? Reflect on your current choices in the following areas and write down their impact.
   • Food
   • Work or career
   • Transportation

- Shopping
- Waste and trash
- Living environment

5. Harmlessness and your relationship to your inner environment.

An important aspect of the practice is to inquire into the motives and intentions behind harmful thoughts and behaviors. If the deep causes and underlying beliefs are not addressed, the behaviors will keep returning in ever new variations.

Take some time this week when you notice a tendency toward being harmful, to pray, contemplate, and inquire into the source of the urges. Helpful questions can be:

- What am I really feeling?
- Do I have a personal need that requires my acknowledgement?
- What is the greater learning or higher truth in this situation?

Prayer enters in by asking for the truth of the situation to be revealed, and by offering God our willingness to change. Write about any clearer understanding that comes to you this week as you explore this process.

6. Change what you can and pray for assistance to change that which you have been unable to change, to bring you into true harmlessness with yourself, others, and our world.

Truthfulness (Satya)

> Ordinary mind perceives surface truths, but enlightened mind sees the inner Truth that doesn't change.
>
> —Baba Hari Dass

The Absolute level of Truth is eternal, not subject to change or modification.

Truth may be defined as that which is. Truth exists at both the absolute and relative levels. The absolute level of Truth is that which is eternal, not subject to change or modification. Supreme Consciousness is Truth, or Absolute Reality. It is beyond change, beyond phenomena, without beginning or end. Relative truth is our own truth based on our individual perception. The thoughts and feelings we express are relative truth since they are subject to change. The way we feel about someone or something in the moment, while true, is changed and transformed as conditions change and new perception arises. Truthfulness practice is the cultivation of awareness of one's divine nature as Supreme Consciousness. It is bringing thought, word, and action into harmony with this awareness. Thus truthfulness is the path to discovering and expressing one's authentic Self.

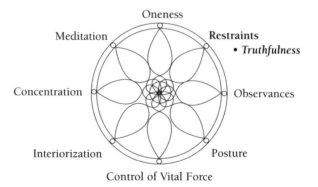

Oneness

Meditation

Restraints
• *Truthfulness*

Concentration

Observances

Interiorization

Posture

Control of Vital Force

Truth means the fulfillment of our self.
—Confucianism

To be truthful in thought, word, and deed requires integrity of being. It requires a quiet mind, a surrendered heart, and a willingness to listen to the guidance that comes from the still small voice of the soul. It allows one to be "in harmony with the Tao" or Spirit. When we are following through on soul guidance, we are living the path of truthfulness.

When we are established in truthfulness, the divine creative energy of Spirit flows through us at the soul level as inspiration then into manifest creation through our thoughts, words, and actions. To live in Truth is "energy efficient." Nothing blocks this flow of energy from the Source; it is infinitely renewable, and our actions are grounded in what is essential and correct.

Truthfulness and Courage

A certain amount of fearlessness is required to live truthfully. At the deepest level, it is the willingness to trust the divine will or the divine plan for our lives. At the times we are ruled by ego, we fear that to stop and truly listen to inner guidance would require us to do something that we do not want to do. The ego or small self has made an investment in a life plan to which we are attached. "I" want this or that. A lack of willingness to surrender to God is accompanied by a fear that this surrender will require giving up what one "wants." This fear is based on the spiritual ignorance of falsely identifying with the body/mind as the self.

Living truthfully requires the willingness to trust the divine will or the divine plan for our lives.

When we comprehend that our very life is God's own, we will understand that what the divine will requires is the very thing that's best for the soul. It will be that which is necessary to bring forth the bliss natural to the soul's authentic expression. When people are established in truthfulness, they are not pulled to act under the influence of such mistaken beliefs as thinking they exist apart from the Source of all life.

Even in our social environment the practice of truthfulness requires courage. Many cultural, social, and political situations are environments where truth is neither practiced nor welcomed. Corruption and hypocrisy are woven into advertising and political messages. Truth seems far from the kinds of messages one hears and reads on a daily basis. There is some expectation that, in order to be socially acceptable, one will "be nice" or "save face" even if it means lying. To find a way to practice truthfulness in such an environment, one must discern what is true and what is not and when it is important to speak out.

I honor those who try to rid themselves of any lying, who empty the self, and have only clear Being there.
—*Rumi*

Truthfulness and Harmlessness

The practice of truthfulness requires one to be ever mindful of the power of words. With every word spoken, energy is put into motion.

It is our responsibility to discern how to implement the interaction of truthfulness and harmlessness.

Words can have the power to heal and to bless. They also have the power to wound. Truth which can harm others is considered best left unspoken. There is an interdependent relationship between the practices of truthfulness and harmlessness.

Truthfulness must be followed in harmony with the virtue of harmlessness. The two virtues are said to work together like the wings of a bird, allowing us to soar to great spiritual heights. Without the two working in harmony, one is led led further into bondage.

One must prayerfully consider how to implement the harmonious interaction of truthfulness and harmlessness. There is not a "rule" which tells us what to do in each instance; it is our responsibility to discern.

A story that is interpreted differently by two teachers will help to illustrate this point.

> A sage is living in a hut in the forest. He is hiding a deer inside. A hunter passing by asks the sage if he has seen the deer. The sage knows that to reveal the deer's whereabouts to the hunter is to bring about the death of the deer since the hunter will kill it. What should he do?

One teacher says: The sage can speak the truth by denying that he has seen the deer. In this case, the sage is following the path of ahimsa or non-violence. In respecting the deer's right to life and not acting to allow violence, the sage has saved himself from complicity in violence which is non-truth.

Another teacher says: This produces conflict because to tell the truth would cause harm to the deer and to lie would break the vow of truthfulness, therefore silence is the truthful response. This teacher suggests that one must do everything in their power to avoid lying, even to the point of remaining silent.

Practicing Truthfulness

> Just as burning is the nature of fire…truthfulness is the nature of a human being.
>
> —Sri Satya Sai Baba
> *Sai Baba Gita*

Truthfulness practice requires faith and courage. Trusting in the truth is actually trusting in the Self. We must be willing to surrender our sense of separate self and trust in the divine purpose expressing in our lives.

Truthfulness requires practicing self-discipline, meditation, and surrender. One must cultivate a quiet mind to be able to discern not only the highest truth of their own nature but the true intention behind one's actions.

The practices associated with truthfulness are:

1. Meditate on Supreme Consciousness (Truth).

2. Contemplate Truth. Inquire into the nature of Reality. What is Truth?

3. Speak only truth, refrain from lying (which includes lies of omission).

4. Keep agreements with self and others—a broken agreement breaks the bond of trust in a relationship (even with oneself).

5. Live in harmony with your soul's direction. Be willing to follow inner guidance.

Know, speak, and live the truth.

When one begins the practice of truthfulness, one of the most helpful tools is silence—both inner silence and refraining from speaking as much as possible. Silence makes it easier to contemplate and reflect upon our perceptions in a given situation, and to ask: What is my truth here? What is actually occurring? By refraining from speaking, we can take the time to consider our words, and to speak only consciously and deliberately, not in reaction. Much of the falsehood spoken can be unintentional, when one is simply not "awake"—not speaking and living with full consciousness.

Silence is a helpful tool for the practice of truthfulness.

It is also helpful to one's practice to "stand guard at the door of your mind." Standing guard at the door of the mind means to not allow falsehood to enter your consciousness. Refrain from listening to harmful speech, gossip, or falsehoods. Do not participate in speaking that is not clear in its intent such as innuendo or sarcasm. Similarly, do not participate in idle chatter, talk for the sake of talk. Practice silence.

Power of Truthfulness

> For one grounded in truthfulness, words acquire the
> power of fulfillment.
>
> —*Yoga Sutra*

*The power associated
with truthfulness is
the power to manifest
one's word.*

The power associated with truthfulness is the power to manifest one's word. It is related to one's direct connection with the divine Truth and the ability to bring forth the divine will on earth. This can be observed in the lives of the great ones whose words were spoken with divine power. When Jesus says of the young girl, "she is not dead, she is sleeping," the girl is healed. It can be thought of this way—there is no interference from the ego self. The words are spoken directly from the divine Self and are, at once, true.

For the seeker on the path beginning this practice, there is usually a realization that one has been somewhat "lazy" when it comes to staying awake and always speaking, thinking, and acting truthfully. It is easy to develop habits of not being completely truthful in speech and not being mindful of following through on agreements.

What happens when we lack the discipline of truthfulness practice is that we actually do not believe in ourselves. Why should we? If we continually say things that we do not really mean, even things we consider unimportant, after a while, we no longer listen to or believe in the power of our own words. The power of the word is a divine, creative power. To speak untruthfully is to lose touch with this gift and to be out of touch with who we are.

In the study of yoga, not much emphasis is put on the potential miraculous powers to be found through truthfulness. The emphasis is placed more strongly upon the intrinsic value of living consciously, speaking truthfully, and practicing harmlessness. However, it is said that when one is accomplished in this practice, one's words will be heard by their students in such a way as to have transforming power. If such a teacher says to a student, "you will be virtuous," or "you will find peace," those words of truth are said to travel straight to the heart of the student with a manifesting power because they resonate with a truth that is already present in the student's greater Being.

PREPARING THE WAY

1. Practice speaking only truth.

   Notice the tendency to exaggerate or to say what you do not actually feel. If you have spoken untruthfully, correct it.

2. Meditate daily.

   Direct your attention within to the clear (Truth) aspect of your own being.

3. Inventory broken agreements.

   List any broken agreements you currently have with yourself or others. Make a plan for clearing them up.

4. Be aware of the interaction of truthfulness and harmlessness.

   Notice the way that truthfulness and harmlessness must interact. Be conscious of harmonizing the two. What happens if either one is sacrificed?

   Write down any situations you are aware of where speaking your truth will bring harm to another.

Non-Stealing (Asteya)

You shall not steal.

—*Torah*, 8th commandment

To practice non-stealing is to dwell in the contentment of the completeness of the Self.

To practice non-stealing is to refrain from taking anything that belongs to another and to be free of envy, desiring anything that is not one's own. With the practice of non-stealing one considers what is theirs by right of consciousness, or what has come to them through their own energy and effort. Therefore, if one finds something such as a sum of money, it is considered stealing to keep it. One should attempt to return it to its rightful owner.

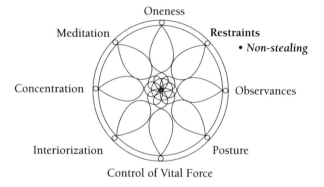

Non-stealing also means to possess only what we need. Excessive acquiring and over-consumption of goods upset the balance of life on this planet by taking resources others may need. Practicing non-stealing does not limit our prosperity; it invites us to be fully conscious of what we truly use.

At the deepest level of spiritual realization, to practice non-stealing is to dwell in the contentment of the completeness of the Self, in which nothing outside of one's own being is desired to bring satisfaction.

Everything Belongs to God

Everything that exists is a manifestation of the Divine, thus everything "belongs" to God. Therefore, non-stealing is also a practice of understanding that we cannot really "own" anything and that our life work is to surrender everything to the Source. This "giving back" process means to give God our love—our attention, our time, and the focus of our life activity. By surrendering what we do to the Source, we are not "stealing" (taking that which does not truly belong to us), but giving back the life that is given to us to its true "owner." For example, for some in the Jewish faith, it is considered "stealing" if one neglects to give thanks before a meal. One has taken something that God has given without giving anything back. This consciousness of rightful ownership is gratitude.

If the only prayer you say in your whole life is 'thank you,' that would suffice.
—Meister Eckhart

True Prosperity

> One who is grounded in non-stealing experiences the jewel of abundance.
>
> *—Yoga Sutra*

Complete reliance on the Self without grasping at externals for security brings true prosperity. When one is Self-realized, needs are provided for effortlessly through harmonious relationship with Life. Such people live by wisdom and are free of the need to chase after anything. All that is needed is sourced within their own consciousness.

When one is Self-realized, needs are provided for effortlessly through harmonious relationship with Life.

Desire and the Fulfillment of Desire

It is possible to see that as long as one is engaged in stealing, in desiring, and in grasping after what belongs to others, there can never be the experience of contentment that comes with true prosperity. Such a person continually lives with the feeling that they do not have enough. Somehow, more is always needed to make them happy. As long as this is the thought process, the experience of actually having enough will not occur.

The flames of desire are not put out by increased desire nor by the fulfillment of desire. Desire and the fulfillment of desire only create more desire.

Vying for more and more diverts you.
—The Koran

Contentment

To find freedom from the bondage of desire, the devotee must discover the fulfillment that is inherent to the soul nature. When one is in contact with the bliss of the soul, nothing further is desired. Happiness is the true nature of the soul. Here one finds freedom from needing anything external for fulfillment. When we are content in the soul nature, all that is needed is provided effortlessly from the Source.

Know the bliss of the soul and overcome desire.

Whenever one experiences that they have and "are" "enough," when the frantic grasping of desire is soothed by the wisdom of the soul, then true prosperity can be experienced. This allows a vantage point of inner peace, where one can see clearly when opportunities arise what the right course of action should be.

Life naturally brings forth what is needed to prosper itself. As we live in the flow of life's natural tendency toward thriving, right action and prosperity go hand in hand. One is able to live with ease, allowing the natural course of events to unfold without the unrest that comes from stealing, grasping, and envy. One can experience that it is natural to prosper, and to be successful in all ways.

When one is established in non-stealing, free of desire and covetousness, that person is continually gifted by life. With such freedom, we naturally draw to ourselves the abundance from the Source that is unlimited.

Practicing Non-Stealing

Refrain from taking anything that does not rightfully belong to you

This would, of course, begin with not stealing things—not shoplifting, or stealing from others in any way.

In a more subtle way, stealing in our culture may take such forms as taking supplies from one's office for personal use, using the office telephone for personal calls, neglecting to return an overpayment of change, lying on the reporting of income for taxes, and so on. Some people rationalize that they are taking things because they are under-paid or in some other way "due." When the stealing is stopped then the underlying cause of the dissatisfaction can be addressed.

Refrain from incurring debt

The practice of using credit cards to purchase things beyond one's ability to afford them is a form of stealing. Such practices also lack truthfulness and contribute to the harmful effects of over-consumption on our planet.

Being in debt ultimately infringes upon one's vital force and freedom and is therefore harmful to the self as well. Debting can occur in other forms of energy besides money, such as pushing your physical body beyond its energy limits—not resting when the body needs rest.

Be conscious about the practice of borrowing

If things are borrowed in good faith, they should be faithfully returned. Neglecting to return things is taking things that do not rightfully belong to you.

Practice generosity

Understanding that all is freely given to us from Spirit, we participate in the divine creative process by becoming conduits for good in the world. The practices of giving our time, energy, and resources to serve God are part of awakening to the abundance of the Divine Presence that prospers us. Whenever we hold back, hoarding when we could rightfully share or give, we are stealing from life, calling "mine" what is not really "ours" but on loan from God. One who feels they cannot give, no matter how much they have, will never experience prosperity.

If I give this, what will I enjoy?—
this selfish thinking is the way of ghosts;
If I enjoy this, what can I give?—
this selfless thinking is the way of the gods.
—Shantideva

Pursue One's Own Work

Non-stealing also can be thought of in terms of pursuing one's own work in the world. If we do the work of another, we are essentially taking their place and not doing that which we have come here to do.

> It is better to do one's own work, even if imperfectly, than to do the work of another, even if done perfectly.
>
> *—Bhagavad Gita*

> Your work is to discover your work and with all of your heart to give yourself to it.
>
> *—Dhammapada*

> Work is worship.
>
> —Virashaiva Proverb

✎ Preparing the Way

Explore the following:

1. Non-stealing and your relationship to taking things.

   Become aware of any areas in your life where you take things that do not rightfully belong to you and stop all such behaviors. If there is a need for amends, write your commitment to repay the person or organization you have taken from.

2. Non-stealing and your relationship to borrowing.

   Make a list of any borrowed items you have that need to be returned, who they belong to, and when you will return them.

3. Non-stealing and your relationship to giving.

   Do you regularly give of your time, money, and service to useful causes?

   What percentage of your income do you give to spiritual or charitable work?

   Do you experience yourself as generous or fearful of giving?

   If you are not currently sharing your resources, begin doing so on a regular basis. Give with the conscious awareness that you are giving to the Source from the Source.

4. Non-stealing and your relationship to incurring debt.

Do you use credit cards for convenience and pay them regularly in full or do you use them to buy beyond what you can actually afford? How do you use loans?

Make a fearless inventory of your financial status and practices. List all your bank and store credit cards and the amount you currently owe each. Also, list any outstanding loans. Cross out any amount you can pay in full in the next 30 days. Add up any remaining amounts.

Credit Card or Loan	Amount Currently Owed	Am I able to pay it in full?	Pay off plan
Total Amount in Debt			
Overall Plan:			

If you are in debt, stop using credit cards immediately. Write an overall plan to become debt-free, or write a payoff plan or date beside each outstanding debt. Include paying off your mortgage in your long term planning. Credit counseling may be helpful in some cases.

5. Non-stealing and your relationship to your work in the world.

Do you feel that you are currently in your right place in life, doing the work that you have come here to do?

If you know that your current work is not right for you, pray for guidance and begin to make the necessary steps to change. It is important to appreciate the current situation where we are, no matter what it is.

The practice of contentment even in challenging situations helps to clear the mind and consciousness so that guidance can be forthcoming and the right opportunities for change can be seen.

If you are aware that you are in your right place, doing what you have come here to do, rejoice! Make yourself increasingly available, through prayer and meditation, to divine inspiration and guidance.

Practice the affirmation "I am now in my right place, guided by divine inspiration. Moment to moment, I live in joy." If you feel you are currently in your right place this affirmation will deepen the experience and bring forth joyful appreciation. If you feel you are not currently in your right place, practicing the affirmation will begin the process of opening in consciousness to the right situation. Since our lives unfold from within, we must first seek the "right place" in consciousness. We are in our right place in consciousness when we recognize our oneness with the Source. From this recognition, clear guidance and right action can proceed.

RIGHT USE OF VITAL FORCE (BRĀHMĀCĀRYĀ)

> It is within my power either to serve God or not to
> serve Him. Serving Him, I add to my own good and
> the good of the whole world. Not serving Him, I
> forfeit my own good and deprive the world of that
> good, which was in my power to create.
>
> —Leo Tolstoy

Vital force is the conscious energy of Spirit that gives life to the soul.
It is the animating principle of our being. Drawing upon this energy,
we exist and carry out all of the functions of the body/mind. The right
use of vital force is the appropriate use of our life energy—in the
forms of our time, attention, and vital energy or resources—in
harmony with the divine purpose for our life. When we are living
according to divine guidance, expressing the soul's purpose in
thought, word, and action, then we are appropriately using our vital
force.

Appropriate use of life force is our use of time, attention, and resources in harmony with the divine purpose for our life.

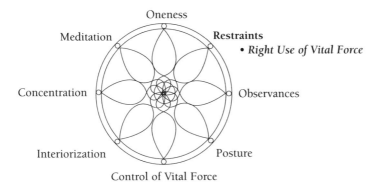

Right use of vital force, at the core of the practice, is concerned
with appropriate channeling of the energy of our life toward our life
purpose. It is concerned with not allowing our vital energy to be
depleted or dispersed, but to remain pure (i.e. singular) in one's spiritual focus.

Those who consciously incline the direction of their life energy
in harmony with their soul destiny will live and pass from this lifetime with a sense of deep fulfillment. Those who do not monitor their

A man is allowed to follow the road he wishes to pursue.
—Talmud

life energy are apt to lose much of the vital energy of this lifetime through dissipation. Simply going through life, unconscious of the precious opportunity for awakening that this incarnation brings, one can literally miss the opportunity of a lifetime.

We do hear stories of those, who at the time of their death, express their regrets at how they wasted their time and energy on pursuits that were ultimately unimportant. How fortunate we are to be exposed to the spiritual path, and to have the opportunity to make the most of our time in this world.

Various Vital Force Definitions

> One established in purity obtains great vitality.
>
> *—Yoga Sutra*

Schools of yoga philosophy define the right use of vital force variously. Some maintain that celibacy is required while others see right use of vital force as the appropriate use of sexual energy as well.

For those who are in committed intimate relationships, sexual involvement in harmony with the right use of vital force is a sexuality dedicated to spiritual purposes. It is dedicated to loving and being loved, to developing compassion, greater awareness, and to experiencing the sacred nature of the body/mind temple. In the sexual act, one's self and one's partner are treated as expressions of the Divine.

Those of the bhakti inclination experience their partner as an aspect or manifestation of their relationship with the Divine Beloved. Those inclined in the direction of the yogas of technique may explore the awakening of vital force and the experience of divine union that can be encouraged through conscious sex, an aspect of Tantra Yoga.

Role of Celibacy

Brahmacarya traditionally refers to the practice of chastity or refraining from sexual activity, which goes beyond simply stopping sexual action. It refers to a harnessing of one's vital energy for the purpose of spiritual enlightenment. This means that one does not allow their energy and attention to be dissipated through sexual desire. The primal human sexual urge, for the dedicated yogi, is transmuted in favor of a single spiritual focus.

Celibacy is one option among others on the spiritual path, and for some devotees it is the correct one. The path of celibacy is often one chosen in combination with the monastic environment. It is important to remember that no spiritual practice will make an individual spiritual, enlightened, or holy. One must find the spiritual practice that is appropriate to their own temperament, time, and soul destiny.

One must find the spiritual practice that is appropriate to their own temperament, time, and soul destiny.

Practicing Right Use of Vital Force

Through the practice of right use of vital force one can directly observe and experience what increases vital force and what dissipates or depletes it.

Vital force is decreased through excessive talking, worrying, meaningless activity, rajasic or tamasic environments—environments that are toxic, that agitate or stress the body, mind, and soul.

Vital force is increased through meditation and devotional practices, silence, living in harmony with one's deepest values, rest, consciously surrendering one's will to the divine will, and spending time in sattvic environments such as nature.

Meditation

Meditation practice promotes the inner quality of clarity that allows one to re-direct attention at will, thus preserving vital force rather than scattering it in external and internal distractions. Through meditation practice, one becomes more aware of both outer and inner environments. With increased sensitivity, one learns to follow inner guidance and to consciously choose what nurtures the soul.

As one meditates, the body/mind is infused with pure energy of Superconsciousness.

Meditation and prayer also allow the devotee to seek renewed energy or the enhancement of vital force directly from the Source. As one meditates, the body/mind is infused with the pure energy of Superconsciousness. This pure energy of Spirit, flowing unobstructed into the system, brings healing and rejuvenation.

Harmony with One's Values

Living in harmony with one's values can be a useful way to think of right use of vital force. When we live in harmony with our own deep values, there is no confusion blocking our field of energy. There is the opportunity for a clear flow of energy from soul to mind and into action.

The work on values clarification developed by Louis Raths and Sidney Simon explores the process of how individual values are established. An established value has the following three components:

A true value has three components.

1. It is prized, cherished, and chosen freely.
2. It is publicly affirmed or acknowledged.
3. It is expressed by some regular action.

When people feel or think that something is of value to them and they cherish it and even publicly acknowledge it but do not take regular action to honor it, it is not considered a developed value but rather an indication of something that may be valued. When our actions are out of harmony with our thoughts and feelings, our energy does not flow freely.

Our work in the world is our opportunity to fulfill the soul's destiny and to be of service to Divine Purpose.

To consistently feel that we value something while being unable or unwilling to affirm it or take regular action on behalf of that value brings great internal stress. One can experience dissatisfaction with life and low energy as a result. There remains a constant inner sense of disquiet or discontent. Conversely, when we are able to fully express our true values, we experience a sense of peace, and inner fulfillment.

Right vocation arises out of the combined practices of harmlessness, truthfulness, and right use of vital force. Our work in the world is our opportunity to fulfill the soul's destiny and to be of service to the Divine Purpose.

Living the Surrendered Life

This practice requires considerable patience, the willingness to wait for inner guidance.

One of the most significant aspects of the right use of vital force is learning to live a surrendered life. Living a surrendered life refers to the willingness to surrender the desires of the ego-driven self to the inner guidance of the higher true Self. This requires spending time in prayer and meditation. It requires taking time to become quiet, and to listen to the prompting of the soul nature as it is revealed within. This practice also requires considerable patience, the willingness to wait for inner guidance.

Living the surrendered life, one learns to work "in consciousness" rather than trying to force external circumstances to change.

The most important spiritual practice here is to give the fullness of one's attention to the divine Presence and to allow right action to arise from within, or to present itself outwardly through synchronicity.

With patience, one can overcome the driven nature of the ego self by learning to recognize its push for urgent action as a sign to slow down a bit, a sign to take the time to pray and consider what the right course of action should be. While there are occasionally valid times in emergency situations requiring quick action, there is rarely the need to act with the haste and urgency that the desire-driven ego tends to favor.

In relationships, when we are surrendered to God, we have the patience to resolve conflicts peacefully and lovingly. One of the most useful tools for fostering healthy relationships is to learn not to attempt to negotiate with another when the emotions are unsettled. This is not a time when people can think clearly or perceive inner guidance very well. It is a skill to learn to let the intensity of emotion subside, then direct attention to the matters at hand.

In the *Tao Te Ching* (translation by Stephen Mitchell) it is written:

> Do you have the patience to wait till your mud settles and the water is clear?
>
> Can you remain unmoving till the right action arises by itself?

The virtue of right use of vital force also requires courage, as one must be willing to live with uncertainty. One must be willing to wait until the knowledge of truth and right action arises.

Honoring the Sabbath: Sacred Rest

The spiritual practice of honoring the Sabbath is helpful for maintaining the right use of one's vital force, especially in our modern world. So much emphasis is placed on work that one can easily spend most of their vital force consumed by work and work-related thoughts and activities. This barely leaves time and energy for one's devotional practices, which are the most important part of life. Everything one accomplishes at work will one day be gone but the gains one makes in awakening last forever.

Do you have the patience to wait till your mud settles and the water is clear?
—Tao Te Ching

Some suggestions for honoring the Sabbath day are:

Set aside a regular 24 hour period where you do not work, plan for work, or think about work. If thoughts of work come to mind, simply set them aside as you would intrusive thoughts during meditation.

*In the remembrance
of God do hearts find
satisfaction.*
—Koran

Begin and end the time period with a prayer of dedication. Light a candle, chant, say prayers of celebration and blessing.

Let the focus of your Sabbath be on receiving the gift of Divine Presence. It is not a time to work on spiritual matters, or to ask for anything in prayers. It is a time to be content, to rest in the awareness of the presence of God.

Celebrate Divine Presence in your life by being with family members—sharing a special meal together, going for a walk, making love with your spouse.

Do whatever is uplifting for you, which helps you experience the joyful nature of being alive.

Attend worship services and enjoy spiritual community.

*Give yourself time
to create a Sabbath
ritual that is right
for you.*

Give yourself time to create a Sabbath ritual that is right for you. The practice of honoring the Sabbath is like going on a meditation retreat—it takes time to adjust. Sometimes people do not know what to do. Sometimes they experience feelings coming up that they haven't had time to feel all week long. The more you practice honoring the Sabbath as a regular discipline the more you will look forward to it as a spiritually fulfilling time.

124

PREPARING THE WAY

1. Begin to bring awareness to the flow of vital force in your life.

   What do you notice increases your vital force?

   What is draining to your vital force?

   Adjust your activities and practice re-directing your energy at will.

2. Spend time in nature this week.

   Write down what you noticed about your energy, before, during, and after your time in nature.

3. Plan and implement a day of silence for yourself.

   During this time, extend your regular time for meditation. Cultivate inner silence in meditation and quiet activity throughout the day. Besides refraining from speech, refrain from exposing yourself to the noise of television, radio, and all that detracts from deliberate, intentional mindfulness.

   Write down what you noticed during the time of silence and after it was over.

4. Observe your relationship to work and the time you make available for worship.

As you explore creating a Sabbath time in your life be aware that this practice requires a commitment over a period of time since it will take a while to establish your boundaries with yourself and the tendency to continually "work" or be involved in some form of doing. A year is a minimum time commitment suggested for learning this spiritual practice.

Write down the first two steps you will take for creating a Sabbath time.

1.

2.

If you determine your course

With force or speed,

You miss the way of the law.

Quietly consider

What is right and what is

wrong.

—Sayings of the Buddha

from the *Dhammapada*

The weekly choice to dedicate one day not to the shopping mall, not to the television or telephone or computer, not to the consciousness of the market, opens the possibility for sacred time in which the call of God can be heard.

—Michael Lerner

Non-Attachment (Aparigraha)

> Use all of your power to free the senses from attach-
> ment and aversion alike, and live in the full wisdom
> of the Self.
>
> —*Bhagavad Gita*

Attachment is said to be the root of all suffering. People assume the unreal to be the Real, able to bring them true fulfillment, security, or satisfaction. It is not that objects, people, or situations in the manifest world are unreal in the sense of having no reality or existence. Things are real in this world. They do exist. It is simply that they have no independent existence. They cannot exist alone. Independent of the power of Spirit, nothing can exist or cause anything. Everything exists only through the life or power of Spirit, the ultimate Reality. The true source of all of our happiness, fulfillment, and security is therefore, Spirit.

Everything exists only through the life or power of Spirit, the ultimate Reality.

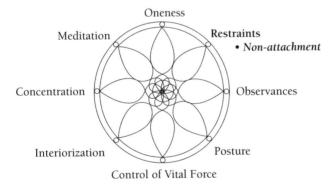

Oneness

Meditation

Restraints
• *Non-attachment*

Concentration

Observances

Interiorization

Posture

Control of Vital Force

Through assigning the potential fulfillment of one's needs and desires to various objects outside of one's self, attachment is produced and greed results. To be established in the virtue of aparigraha is to be free from greed. Aversion (i.e., that which one is "attached to" or intent upon avoiding) has the same binding effect.

Identification With Objects of the Senses
Through the process of identification, one assumes something outside

of the self is an extension of the self, erroneously assigning the power of the soul to the external object. This produces attachment to the object, as one believes one's own well-being depends upon the object. This belief may be mild, as when we own and appreciate certain possessions we do not consider essential, or severe, as with possessions or relationships we may believe that we cannot exist, or survive, without.

Attachment and Our Feelings of Joy and Security

Lasting joy exists within the Self.

It is difficult to discern the truth about the nature of Reality and the nature of attachment because as we experience the world, it seems as if things outside of ourselves do have the ability to bring us happiness, or security. We notice that we feel happy or fulfilled when we have certain things and we feel sad without them. Doesn't this mean that those things have brought us that happiness or that security? The answer, while not the obvious one, is no.

Identification with the objects of the senses is produced as a result of falsely ascribing one's joy or one's security to the object. All joy and all security resides within the Self. When we imagine that our joy comes from something outside of the Self, we have "identified" with that outside element. This identification produces confusion and bondage as one searches endlessly in the world in an attempt to find lasting joy.

Lasting joy and security exist only within the Self. Any joy or security perceived in the manifest realm is a reflection of the joy (bliss) or the security (eternal existence) of the Self.

When we have identified our own security (existence) and happiness (bliss) with objects, whether relationships, situations, or actual physical things outside our Self, and those things change, suffering is the result.

For example, a woman buys a new car. She feels the happiness she associates with having this vehicle she has desired. She may even feel an associated lift in her self-esteem, which she attributes to having a better automobile and an improved image in the world. She enjoys driving the car and being seen in this car. What happens when there is an accident, and the new car is damaged? What was once perceived as a source of happiness now becomes a source of sorrow, or suffering.

Attachment in Relationship

Attachment in relationships prevents us from seeing clearly and produces false perceptions of gain and loss of our inherent happiness. In relationships, with attachment to the other as the source of one's happiness or security, the problem is compounded. Not only does one person suffer as a result, but both are subject to suffering from this attachment.

If someone is attached to another as their source of happiness or security, they have identified with that individual and in a sense, robbed them of their individuality. The "loved" one in this type of relationship is objectified, seen as an extension of what is needed to bring personal satisfaction. When this happens, there is an implicit request in the relationship for one's partner to confine their own growth in such a way that it accords with the needs of the other. The message, whether conscious or unconscious is: "don't change" from ways that please me, or "change" to make me happy.

True love in relationship is not attachment to the other as a source of happiness or security. It is the ability to love the Divine in one's partner. When we are able to love the Divine in another, we love the way in which they grow and change, the ways in which they are ever becoming more of their authentic Self.

If we are not attached to another, we can appreciate their changes; we do not need them to be a certain way in order for us experience fulfillment or happiness. One established in non-attachment relies solely on the true Self and has no need to grasp for externals as a means of providing security.

True love in relationship...is the ability to love the Divine in another.

Practicing Non-Attachment

Non-attachment to possessions, people, or circumstances

This practice coincides with non-stealing, harmlessness, and right use of vital force. Non-attachment to possessions, people, or circumstances is cultivated through:

- Realizing the defects inherent in all things

  The word "defects" is used to indicate that all things fall short of being perfect. Perfection is possible only with that which is eternal, i.e. the

Self. Anything else is subject to change and subject to decay over time.

• Releasing ideas of "me" and "mine" and practicing generosity

Consider what it is possible to really own. Where do things originate? What sustains them? Contemplate Spirit as the rightful Cause and Sustainer of all that exists.

Simplicity, which has no name, is free of desires. Being free of desires, it is peaceful.
—Tao Te Ching

• Simplifying one's lifestyle

In our modern lifestyles it is so easy to come to "depend" upon certain things. It is easy to forget that these modern conveniences are not the source of our well-being. Simplifying one's lifestyle helps to free our attention to be able to discern and to focus upon that which is truly relevant in our life.

• Re-directing outer-directed urges to inner focus

Meditate more. Increased meditation will reveal the self-contained joy of the Self. In the light of the Self, desires will fade. One can actually observe them arise and pass away.

• Cultivating healthy relationships by learning to love and honor the Divine in others

Practice supporting others' full development, letting go of any attachments to them needing to be a certain way in order to please you.

Realize that God is the Cause and the Manifestation, and all belongs to God.

Non-attachment to the results of one's actions

For this practice, one is active in the world and works with integrity, doing all they are led to do while surrendering the outcome to God. There is no attachment to the result of the work that one does.

Sometimes people imagine that this practice leads to an unhealthy indifference toward what one is engaged in. They are concerned that to be non-attached to the results of one's actions is not to care about what one does. The opposite is true. With non-attachment, one cares about their work because it is an offering to God. It is, in a sense, a form of worship. When we are spiritually non-attached to outcomes, it is because we realize that God is the Cause, and the Manifestation, and that all belongs to God. The core of non-attachment is the realization that God is the doer.

Non-attachment does not mean giving up one's work or family and going into a "cave" in the wilderness to live as a literal renunciate. It is being in the world but not of it. It is learning to live in the "cave of one's heart," to continually dwell in the Self through surrender, through offering to the Divine what one is and does. This requires letting go of all attachment to the results.

You have the right to work, but never to the fruit of work.
—Bhagavad Gita

> Detachment does not mean indifference; it is correctly called "holy indifference"—neither inaction nor reaction, but real, positive action with a balanced mind.
>
> —S.N. Goenka

This practice frees one from the bondage of karma through the release of personal desire and attachment to actions. When we have strong desires about the outcome of what we do, we tie ourselves, our happiness or lack of it, to something external. We also bind ourselves to further action through our desires and interfere with our ability to receive clear guidance from the soul.

Non-attachment to the body

> One who is grounded in non-attachment acquires knowledge of the cycles of birth and death.
>
> —*Yoga Sutra*

Most people do not remember their birth or know the time of their death. This is ironically due to attachment to the physical body. Because as spiritual beings we are eternal, we cannot imagine a time when we did not exist. This is true. However, we tend to mistakenly identify our eternal Self with the physical body, therefore we cannot imagine a time before the body existed or a time when it will cease to exist. This threatens what we have come to identify (falsely) as our own existence. When attachment to the body is withdrawn and one resides in the eternal Self, it then becomes possible to know the process of one's birth and death in this and other lifetimes. This is an ability of many saints and enlightened beings who not only remember their entrance into this world, but accurately predict their time of death as well.

Non-attachment to views

Do not think the knowledge you presently possess is changeless, absolute truth...Learn and practice non-attachment from views in order to be open to receive others' viewpoints.

—Thich Nhat Hanh
From the second precept of Interbeing

Through the relinquishment of desire, immortality is realized.

We can continually receive new inspiration and information in life. If we become attached to our ideas or viewpoints, we impede our ability to receive fresh knowledge. We interfere with the ongoing process of illumination and with being able to receive guidance from Spirit.

This side of the Transcendental Realm (ultimate unchanging Reality), there is ever-new possibility. We can only be open to that possibility if we let go of our attachment to thinking that we are "right" or that our current understanding is the only truth.

The pressing need to be "right" about one's views is an indicator of the ego's drive for self-aggrandizement. When we are centered in the conscious awareness of our true Self as spiritual, we are not threatened by the views of others and have no need to insist on our own. We can remain open with the awareness that as people are unique expressions of the one life of Spirit, there are perhaps as many views as there are individual expressions. Most of us can remember a time when we thought we were "right" about something only later to discover we did not have the correct information. In the human condition, our view is always partial. With divine awareness, one's viewpoint is expansive enough to allow even opposite points of view to exist.

PREPARING THE WAY

1. Practice delaying action on carrying out desires.

   Pause to inquire into what you are attracted to. Be aware of the "defects" in the object of your desire.

   • Is what you desire a "want" or a "need"?

   • What do you imagine the fulfillment of this desire will do for you?

   • What would you have gained if your desire was fulfilled and then you later lost it?

2. Practice appreciating the positive qualities inherent in objects and people you are attracted to as qualities of the Divine.

   Recognize the true source of your happiness. Notice how you respond differently at different times to the same person or object. If the happiness or sorrow were inherent in the object, your response would always be the same.

   When you appreciate positive qualities around you, attempt to find or affirm those qualities within yourself.

3. When you disapprove of negative qualities around you, notice your aversion as an opportunity to examine parts of yourself being mirrored in the other, or in the situation or thing.

4. Practice giving with a joyous heart.

   Give service with the awareness that God is acting through you.

List some ideas of where you could donate your time and resources.

5. Practice simplifying your life.

Make a list of what you are not using that might benefit someone else.

Clear away possessions that are not needed.

6. Extend your time of daily meditation.

7. Practice prayerful awareness.

Pray at the beginning, during the performance of, and at the ending of activities.

• At the outset of actions offer the fruits of your labor to God.

• During the performance of your duties, let the mind continually return to the awareness of the presence of God.

• At the completion of the project, give thanks for the opportunity to be of service and surrender all of the outcomes from your activity to God.

> Manifest plainness,
> Embrace simplicity,
> Reduce selfishness,
> Have few desires.
>   —*Tao Te Ching*

CLEANLINESS (SHAUCA)

> Blessed are the pure in heart, for they shall see God.
>
> —Jesus

With this section, we move from the "restraints" to the "observances." The restraints pertain to one's relationship with the world, while the observances are more strongly focused on relationship with the inner Self. Two of the observances, Study of the Nature of Consciousness and Self-discipline, are covered earlier in the text as Contemplation (Part Two, Chapter Five) and Cultivation of the Virtues in the opening pages of this chapter. The next observance is Cleanliness.

By purity of heart alone is the holy Eternal attained.
—Adi Granth

The yogic practice of cleanliness is focused on the recovery of

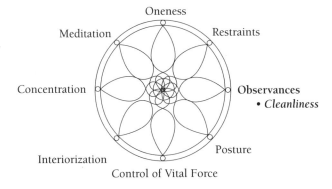

one's natural state of purity. The intention is not to "make" one's self pure but rather to cleanse the body/mind vehicle so that the true, natural purity of the Self is perceived.

If soot covers the glass shade of the lamp, the inner light will not shine through as brightly. Even though the light itself is bright, its appearance is dulled, its brightness hidden. When one's body and mind are filled with toxins, the brightness of the Self is hidden. In some respects, one could say that the true aim of all yoga is this purification, which allows the true Self to be known.

When one's body and mind are filled with toxins, the brightness of the Self is hidden.

To practice cleanliness is to cultivate an environment that is conducive to spiritual realization. Such an environment is sattvic, free from confusion, unrest, or disease. A pure environment is uplifting and nourishing to the soul. We may have the best intentions to practice self-discipline and maintain even-mindedness, but if we continually expose ourselves to environments that are detrimental to spiritual progress, we will fail in our intentions.

One is not always able to maintain control over the influences in both the inner and outer environments, but becoming conscious of such influences expands the possibilities of choice. If one cannot leave or change an environment that is impure, certain cleansing practices can be undertaken to restore equilibrium to the body/mind.

Cleanliness practices like a healing rain, purify the body/mind so the light of the Self shines forth.

There are those who would follow what they consider to be the path of purity, denying the physical world and the physical body. Such aspirants attempt to "rise above" the physical level of existence, developing an aversion to the physical body. Such extreme approaches have been cautioned against by the enlightened ones of all times. The realization of the need for a balanced approach to maintaining the health of the physical body while pursuing one's spiritual path led to the "middle way" teaching of the Buddha.

Cleansing Practices for the Mental Field

> The Yogin practicing cleanliness gets purification of heart which leads to mental bliss, or spontaneous feeling of joy. From mental bliss develops one-pointedness which leads to subjugation of the senses. From subjugation of the organs, Buddhi (pure I-sense) develops the power of realizing the Self. All these are attained by establishment in purification.
>
> —Swami Hariharananda Aranya

Mental purification is the removal from the mind any tendencies which obscure the Self, such as greed, arrogance, attachment, or pride. The following practices contribute to mental purification.

Practice of Superconscious meditation

Superconscious meditation takes place when the initial stages of interiorization and meditation are fulfilled, when awareness rests in the clear aspect of being. In Superconscious meditation, one experiences the Self that is beyond thought activity.

At the conclusion of the time of meditation, focus your attention at the crown chakra (top of the head) and through intention, draw the flow of subtle energy into your mind and body. This exercise works on a subtle level to access and bring clear energy into the body/mind, and to remind us that we can enhance our available subtle energy by drawing directly from the Source.

Some individuals are able to feel this flow of energy. Others perceive it visually as light. Some do not experience the energy at all, but are able to notice a change in their body/mind following their practice. Through this practice, we affirm our ability to nurture ourselves spiritually as well as physically.

The body is cleansed by water, the heart by truthfulness...the intellect by true knowledge.
—Laws of Manu

Chant and pray

Devotion to God cleanses the mental field of pride and self-centeredness. Chanting and prayer open the door to surrender.

Redirect attention

While we cannot control our thoughts by restricting what enters the mind, we can learn to direct our attention toward thoughts and emotions that are useful, and away from those that obscure our mental clarity. The point here is one of emphasis, not control. It is not that one should attempt to think only certain thoughts, rather, we notice where we focus our attention, where we allow the mind to dwell, and choose the sattvic over the rajasic and tamasic thoughts. We become like that which we contemplate and hold in our consciousness.

Direct attention toward that which is useful.

Resist negative influences

"Stand guard at the door of your consciousness" by resisting negative influences (gossip, criticism, violence on TV, etc.). Discipline is needed to remove ourselves from negative situations and influences. There is no need to be harmful, or to unnecessarily educate others about our views. Sometimes, a simple and polite "excuse me" and removing oneself from the situation will suffice.

Seek sattvic environments

Seek out sattvic environments for the mind (uplifting conversations with other devotees on the spiritual path, study of scripture, reading about lives of the saints, etc.).

> Though I had nothing to eat but a red-hot ball of iron, I will never accept the most savory food offered by a person with an impure mind.
>
> Though I were sitting upon a blazing fire hot enough to melt copper, I will never go to visit the place of a person with a polluted mind.
>
> —*Oracle of Hachiman*

Cleansing Practices for the Body

> One of the most important disciplines necessary for coming into union with God is control of the tongue. This must be exercised both in the area of food and in the area of speech. Without control of the tongue it is impossible to follow the path of devotion and become one with God.
>
> —Sri Satya Sai Baba

External Cleansing

Do you not know that your body is a temple of the Holy Spirit within you, which you have from God?
—1 Corinthians 6

Beyond regular bathing hygiene practice, one may also use a brush or loofa to scrub the skin, ridding the body of toxins. This can be especially useful during fasting. Seeing to the cleansing of the physical body is an important part of honoring the body temple as the dwelling place of the divine Self.

Internal Cleansing—Diet

A simple diet is recommended for internal cleansing: one high in fiber, containing foods that are sattvic in nature, and free of toxic chemicals. Organically grown foods are recommended, if available. The cleansing diet consists of three to five days of the following menu:

> Breakfast: fresh fruit, any combination in generous portions.

Lunch: brown rice and fresh green salad of a mixture of greens and raw vegetables (no dressing, lemon juice may be used.)

Dinner: brown rice and salad or steamed vegetables.

Beverages: pure water or herbal teas.

Generous portions are to be eaten at meal times with no snacking between meals. All toxic substances such as alcohol, coffee, sugar, or cigarettes are eliminated during the cleansing diet.

This diet is low in protein, and allows the organs to rest and revitalize through their own natural ability. The high fiber content will cleanse the intestinal tract. As with all diets, individual needs must be taken into consideration and the cleanse must be conducted under the supervision of a medical professional if one has special health conditions.

Internal Cleansing—Fasting

One may also choose a complete fast for 24 hours as a body cleansing practice. Drink only pure water during this time. Be advised that one's entire system becomes sensitized during the cleansing process so it is important to fast during a time when you can be quiet, rest, and meditate.

Do not attempt to fast while keeping up your regular routine; it can be too taxing on the body and does not allow the time for inner reflection significant to the process.

Cleansing and Conscious Awareness

During body cleansing practices, it is helpful to practice mental cleansing and conscious awareness as well. Sometimes food is taken in unconsciously as a habit, when one is not necessarily hungry, in an attempt to satisfy emotional needs. When this habitual pattern is stopped for a time, the emotional needs will surface and there is the opportunity to become conscious of the underlying emotional patterns.

Cleanliness is next to Godliness.
—John Wesley

During the cleansing diet or fast you may notice certain food cravings or moods arising. To practice mental cleansing during this

139

time, notice the craving or mood and inquire into the real nature of the need. Are you really hungry? Unhappy? What does it feel like? Where is the feeling or sensation located in your body? How long does it last when you bring your attention to it? Does it change when you bring your attention to it? After a time of inquiry into the emotion, let the feeling go and turn your attention to the Divine. This practice will provide information about changes you may need to make in your dietary practices and will increase your ability to utilize self-discipline.

Invite in divine grace, by letting go of self-will.

Self-discipline is absolutely essential to higher levels of awareness. If one is continually at the mercy of the desires for sense gratification there will be no peace. Without inner peace, there can be no true realization.

Working with Natural Tendencies

To cultivate such practices as cleanliness, one may need to work with the tendencies in nature in the following way: first, the rajasic tendency is applied to activate and overcome the tamasic tendency. Then, the sattvic tendency is cultivated to bring steadiness to the rajasic tendency.

In practice, this might be understood as initially using willpower to initiate certain spiritual practices. Once the practice is initiated and regulated through the use of will (rajasic energy) then one surrenders the practice and its outcome through prayer and meditation and other sattvic influences. This invites in divine grace, through a letting go of self-will, allowing the spiritual experience to proceed beyond the level of personal will and control.

> One established in purity (cleanliness) abstains from contamination. Through this purity one achieves joy, even-mindedness, detachment, mastery over the senses, and the ability to perceive the true Self.
>
> —*Yoga Sutra*

Cleanliness practice is our spiritual "fitness" practice, the way in which we ready ourselves to receive, through divine grace, the enlightenment experience.

PREPARING THE WAY

1. Become conscious of the condition of your inner and outer environments.

   Are you cultivating a pure environment for yourself, one that is nurturing to your soul? List any areas you are aware of that need improvement.

2. List changes that you can make in your environment that will contribute to serenity and inner peace. Make the necessary changes in your environment.

3. Do an internal cleansing.

   Go on a cleansing diet and/or 24 hour fast. Increase your meditation and rest during this time. Write down your experience and note any changes that you feel would be helpful to you as a result of this experience.

4. Resist negative influences.

   Practice freeing yourself from negative environmental influences and/or using cleansing practices to balance out toxic influences.

For everything there is an appropriate way of polishing; the heart's polishing is the remembrance of God.

—Hadith of Tirmidhi

CONTENTMENT (SĀMTOSHA)

> The first peace, which is the most important, is that
> which comes within the souls of people when they
> realize their relationship, their oneness, with the
> universe and all its powers, and when they realize at
> the center of the universe dwells the Great Spirit,
> and that this center is really everywhere; it is within
> each of us.
>
> —Black Elk

Contentment practice is dwelling continually in remembrance of the true Self.

Contentment practice is dwelling continually in remembrance of the true Self, thereby experiencing the fulfillment that is natural to the soul. At the soul level, we are one with Spirit, ever self-contained, conscious, and free. There is nothing external that needs to be added on in order to be happy. Happiness flows from the inherent bliss of the soul.

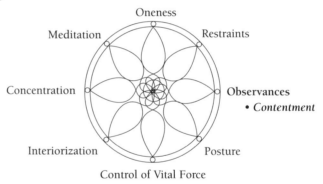

It is significant to note that the experience of unlimited joy is revealed through contentment practice. Most people are accustomed to thinking that once they fulfill certain desires then they will experience joy, peace, and happiness. The sutras clearly instruct us that true joy and lasting happiness are to be found first within the realm of our own consciousness. Find the inner contentment that is natural to the soul and true joy follows, joy that is unshakable!

Through contentment, unlimited joy is realized.

—*Yoga Sutra*

Contentment and the Other Virtues

It is possible to see why contentment practice follows the cultivation of other virtues such as right use of vital force and non-attachment. It is necessary to have a certain degree of peace of mind or inner quiet before one can perceive the bliss of the soul. When the body/mind is in conflict through a lifestyle inconsistent with spiritual values, inner happiness is difficult to access. However, contentment practice can begin in any moment and does not have to wait until all of the other virtues are completely integrated into one's life.

Contentment practice can begin in any moment.

Practicing Contentment

In order to practice contentment one must learn the art of "letting go," which is related to the practice of non-attachment. When we let go with faith, we are trusting the outcome to the Divine. Letting go with faith is very different than letting go in resignation. When we let go with resignation, we lack trust and have given up on happiness. Letting go in resignation is despair. Letting go in faith is contentment.

To experience contentment one must cultivate even-mindedness, being non-reactive to change. We can do this when we are identified with the eternal, unchanging Self. Often much of our life force is spent resisting change. Resistance is hard work! Learning to let go of forcing the outcomes according to our ego-driven desire and yet work joyfully to accomplish useful work in the world is a delicate balance.

The key is surrender. Surrender the outcome to the Divine. Surrender attention inwardly to Divine Presence. This is where contentment is to be found. Nothing that can be achieved in this world can promise more.

The key is surrender.

When to Start Practicing Contentment

The moment to begin and experience contentment is now. Contentment practice is related to living in and being conscious of the present moment. It requires letting go of regrets about the past and worries about the future. The present moment is then recognized as a sacred opportunity to be aware. The present moment is then seen as a bridge that connects our past and our future. With contentment practice, one plants seeds of happiness and peace in the present moment. These seeds contribute to the healing of the past and the flowering of peace in our future.

Wisdom and Contentment

The practice of discernment, or wisdom, is an essential ingredient to understanding the basis for true contentment. How can one do it? How is it possible to be content with so much suffering in our own lives and in our world? There are two primary factors of wisdom that can bring understanding here.

Change is the one thing in the manifest realm that is certain.

Changelessness of the Self

The first factor of wisdom is that we understand our true identity as spiritual beings is greater than any suffering. We place our emphasis on the spiritual aspect of life that remains unharmed and untouched by suffering. Some imagine that this would surely be a kind of indifference, a way of being in life that is disconnected from reality. The important question here is: what is truly real?

Here is a story to illustrate this understanding.

> A farmer purchased a fine horse. All of his neighbors in the village complimented him on this horse and exclaimed how lucky he was. His reply was, "It's too soon to tell." One day his horse disappeared. This time the villagers thought the farmer was very unlucky. They expressed their concern to him and he again replied, "It's too soon to tell." As it turned out, it was! A few days later his horse returned, bringing a wild mare with him. The villagers exclaimed, "How happy you must be!" Again, "Too soon to tell" was the farmer's only reply. The farmer's son set about the task of taming the wild mare and was injured by the horse. After that time he walked with a limp. The villagers remarked upon the farmer's misfortune, to have his only son injured in such a way. "Too soon to tell," he told them. When the war broke out in a neighboring village, the farmer's son, due to his limp, was unable to go. How fortunate, exclaimed the villagers...

With discernment, one realizes that everything in the manifest realm is subject to change. Change is the one thing in the manifest realm that is certain! Why place the power over one's own happiness in such a precarious situation? Have faith in your Self. Experience the contentment of the soul that is unchanging.

I am the Lord, I change not.
—Malachi 3:6

Compassion and Action

The second factor of wisdom one finds in contentment practice is compassion. The question whether dwelling continually in contentment indicates a certain indifference to suffering is important. Indifference to suffering is not spiritually sound. However, being able to feel the suffering of others is only part of the picture. Compassion demands action. When we truly feel the suffering of another, we are moved to help.

Here is where contentment practice comes in. If we allow ourselves to be pulled down by our own suffering and by the suffering of the world, we are generally not able to do much about it. However, if we remain centered in the peace and strength of the true Self, we can find the presence of mind and the energy needed to make necessary changes.

Dwelling in contentment is not the same as "denial." When we deny what is occurring it remains out of our awareness. With contentment practice we are aware of all that is occurring but we make a conscious choice to place the focus of attention on the inner Self. Therefore one dwells in constant peace and is not subject to the ups and downs of changing outer circumstances. This is relying on the Divine. To practice contentment is to live by faith. It is to see through the changing nature of outer phenomena with a willingness to trust and participate in the divine plan.

To practice contentment is to live by faith.

"Live in joy,
In love,
Even among those who hate.
Live in joy,
In peace,
Even among the troubled…"
    —Dhammapada,
(rendering by Thomas Byrom)

145

PREPARING THE WAY

1. Smile.

   The Buddhist monk, Thich Nhat Hanh, suggests the practice of smiling. Smile gently, even in the face of sorrow. This, he says, is a practice of declaring that we are greater than our sorrows. Practice smiling the smile of the Buddha, and dwelling in the realization of your true Self.

2. Acknowledge goodness.

   Look for what is good in yourself, in your life, and in others. Acknowledge this goodness verbally.

3. Record your own "too soon to tell" story.

   Write about a time in your life when things turned out much differently than you expected. How might contentment practice have helped you?

   The restless mind is not fixed at one spot;

   Like a deer it nibbles at tender shoots.

   Should man lodge in mind the divine lotus feet,

   His life span is lengthened, his mind awakened, immortal he becomes.

   All beings are in the grip of anxiety;

   But by contemplation of God comes joy.

   —*Adi Granth*

We awaken to the Divine Presence
within us and around us and continue
to do our duty in this lifetime.

Viewed from the outside
it looks just the same.
But inside—
the soul is singing—
Oh the wood!
Oh the water!

—Ellen Grace O'Brian,
One Heart Opening

Eight
Surrender and Service

Love conquers all things; let us too surrender to Love.
—Virgil

Once the work of building the spiritual foundation is undertaken, the journey of spiritual awakening is begun in earnest. The components of the Fourfold Practice—cultivation of the virtues (restraints and observances), contemplation of the nature of reality, prayer and meditation, and surrendering the sense of separate self—clear the way for the experience of samadhi or oneness with the Divine.

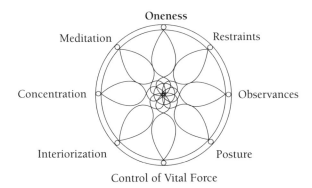

SURRENDER OF THE SENSE OF SEPARATE SELF

The Eternal Way of remembrance of the divine, true Self in our moment-to-moment experience culminates in the surrender of the sense of separate self. With this surrender, one lets go of the struggle of needing to make things happen and opens to the reality of working in harmony with the higher, true Self.

Through surrender of the sense of separate existence (ego), all fears are removed. Fear dwells only within the confines of the ego-self—that part of us which perceives itself to be separate, alone, and limited. From the ego's perspective, life is a continual battle to get needs met, an ongoing competition for survival. When this false sense of separation is released, so is the fear that accompanies it. One then dwells continually in the resourcefulness of the divine Self, experiencing that all needs are met abundantly from moment to moment.

Paradoxically, it is the ego itself that surrenders. A healthy ego is needed to let go, to turn the attention to the higher Self, and to become willing to serve. An unhealthy or unstable ego will want to remain in control, will not be able to surrender, and will resist higher guidance.

Wanting nothing,
With all your heart
stop the stream.
—Buddha

The cultivation of the virtues—the restraints and observances of Eight-Limbed Yoga—combined with the practice of prayer and meditation are the foundation for this letting go and living a surrendered life in God. Without the necessary foundation through self-discipline, contemplation, and meditation, one cannot maintain a life of surrender. The tendency of human nature to get caught in personal desires and distracted by outer circumstances carries away the one who is not awake to spiritual reality.

> Therefore whosoever heareth these sayings of mine, and doeth them, I will liken him unto a wise man, which built his house upon a rock. And the rain descended, and the floods came, and the winds blew, and beat upon that house; and it fell not; for it was founded upon a rock.
>
> —Words of Jesus, from Matthew 7:24-25

The Experience of Oneness

Samadhi is a Sanskrit word used to describe the experience of oneness with Spirit. One may have this experience during meditation, in which all sense of separateness dissolves and what remains is purely the essential Self.

Samadhi experiences have been described variously as being with or without support. The samadhi experience of oneness with support is experiencing oneness with some aspect of the Divine such as light or sound. Oneness without support is the pure experience of Being, or Consciousness beyond any identification.

Saints throughout time in all traditions have described the mystical experience of samadhi, or oneness with God. While these many individuals often lived a virtuous life of prayer and dedication to the Divine, they point out the following paradox. Although their spiritual practices seemed to create a readiness in them, their own efforts did not bring about or cause the experience of samadhi. The experience comes only through divine grace.

The experience of samadhi comes only through divine grace.

> But the nature of this one Reality is such that it cannot be directly and immediately apprehended except by those who have chosen to fulfill certain conditions, making themselves loving, pure in heart, and poor in spirit.
>
> —Aldous Huxley

Grace can be thought of as the divine tendency that moves through all of life as a blessing, bringing it to its natural evolution of awakening in consciousness. While we each live and move and have our being in this "sea of divine grace," we are only aware of it from time to time. The experience of divine grace is revealed in our consciousness according to the divine plan. This divine plan is not related to merit, or earned according to the rational ego plan, but is the unfoldment of divine love in our lives.

What we have in yoga as a spiritual path is the combination of self-discipline and divine grace bringing us to conscious fulfillment.

A beautiful metaphor describes this divine partnership:

The experience of divine grace is not related to merit, but is the unfoldment of divine love in our lives.

> Whenever the devotee raises up one hand to God,
> God reaches down to the devotee with two.

Service is the bridge connecting soul, divine inspiration, and all other beings in Spirit.

The experience of oneness is the true culmination and fulfillment of yoga practice. It is Self-realization.

Spiritual Service

As one progresses on the spiritual path, becoming ever more awake in God, there is a natural tendency to shift from striving to fulfill personal desires to desiring to be of service. As we awaken and sense that our life is imbued with divine purpose, we experience an urge to participate consciously in the divine plan and to do what Spirit intends. We yearn to know this divine purpose and to act in harmony with it.

Along with the yearning to follow the divine plan, there arises compassion, a heartfelt connection to all beings. Our sense of separateness gone, we no longer feel alone.

Service is the bridge connecting our own soul, divine inspiration, and all other beings in Spirit. The step of surrender in service to God is the continual offering of our lives to the Divine. This means opening ourselves to divine inspiration and taking the necessary steps to follow through. Giving one's life to God does not mean that Spirit will do it all, that somehow we will be magically transformed! It means that we cultivate the willingness to act according to divine guidance, to surrender our resistance to the divine plan.

Cultivate the willingness to act according to divine guidance.

An Arab fable tells of a man traveling through the forest one day who comes upon an injured fox. The animal had broken two of its legs and yet continued to live. Wondering how this could be possible, the man hid behind a tree to watch how it was getting its food. What he saw astounded him! A tiger came with game in its mouth. After eating its fill, the tiger left the rest of the meat for the fox to eat. Each day God fed the injured fox through the same tiger. This made the man aware of God's greatness and tender mercy in caring for all creatures. He then reasoned: "I too will show complete trust in God. I will rest here and know that I will be provided with all that I need." After many days without food, and near death from starvation, the man heard a voice cry out: "You who are in error, find the truth! Stop imitating the disabled fox. Open your eyes and follow the example of the tiger!"

On the street I saw a naked child, hungry and shiv-
ering in the cold. I became angry and said to God,
"Why do you permit this? Why don't you do something?" For a while God said nothing. That night
God replied, quite suddenly, "I certainly did something. I made you."

—Anthony de Mello, *The Song of the Bird*

The Process of Conscious Creation

When we surrender to living a life dedicated to following the divine
plan and our own soul's purpose, a natural pattern of manifestation
occurs. This pattern has seven stages, as follows:

1. Connecting with the soul's purpose is made possible   *Soul purpose*
   through one's spiritual disciplines, devotion, and
   divine grace. Once one becomes able to discern soul
   inspiration and guidance, it can be returned to repeat-
   edly and easily.

2. When there is a clear connection at the level of soul,   *Inner guidance*
   inner guidance is accessible. It is possible to inquire
   directly of the soul for guidance. Asking to know what
   is in harmony with one's own soul constitutes a form
   of prayer.

3. Following the guidance of the soul leads one to vision,   *Vision*
   to sensing or seeing the possibilities that can unfold
   from this inner direction. Often, dreams or
   synchronicities will bring more inspiration, clarity, and
   support.

4. Once there is a vision of possibility, the next step is   *Commitment*
   commitment to that vision. The commitment is faith
   in the divine inspiration you have received and the
   promise to act upon it. It is also a commitment to
   continue to be open to this divine guidance as the
   process unfolds, moment to conscious moment.

Self-discipline

5. Taking the necessary action steps toward the realization of a vision requires self-discipline. Especially necessary is the inner directing of the attention to God or Spirit in all that one does, holding to faith in the divine plan. Spiritual practice is the essential foundation for such courageous behavior.

Action

6. Action (thoughts, words, behaviors) is then taken in accordance with inner guidance. The results of guided actions are surrendered to the Divine, without attachment to the outcome. After all, there is a realization from the very beginning that this is God's plan! One's actions are an offering. There is great joy to be experienced in living and acting according to divine guidance in this way.

Manifestation

7. The last stage is manifestation, in which one gives thanks for what has been created in divine co-creation.

LIVING THE SPIRITUAL LIFE

Living the spiritual life is coming home to the truth of our own nature.

The spiritual life holds the secret joy of our own fulfillment. It is easy to see in today's world, with so much material wealth available to many, that true fulfillment is not to be found either in things or in worldly successes. Conversely, true happiness is not necessarily to be found in those lacking in wealth or worldly success.

The spiritual life opens the inner vistas of perception, allowing us to perceive what it is we truly yearn for: nothing other than our own true Self—to be fully alive, to be free, to be conscious, to give and receive love. What we truly want are the qualities of our own soul. And so it is that we search for what is already ours, what we have never been without, what we have never lost.

Living the spiritual life is our way of coming home.

Sit in meditation

The door of the heart opens to the inner world.

After that,

nothing is ever the same.

The knots around your life,

all the reasons for doing and not doing,

loosen and fall away.

Then, there comes the glorious choice.

Some close the door and try to go back

to an anxious way of pretending they don't know.

Others leave the door open and

walk through it to a new life,

full of wonders,

only now perceived.

—Ellen Grace O'Brian,
One Heart Opening

Appendices
Resources for the Path

This spiritual training course is designed for either individual or group participation. The book grew out of exercises used in classes and study groups at the Center for Spiritual Enlightenment.

Unless one has the opportunity to retreat from society for an extended period, spiritual practice occurs in our daily life; in fact it *is* our daily life, inseparable from family, workplace, and community. Consciously forming groups for spiritual focus and support contributes to the awakening and wellness of our planet.

Forming an Eternal Way study group in your community can support the awakening process through the combined commitment of group members to spiritual practice. It also can become a source of inspiration, as you begin to see the activity of Spirit moving in and through the lives of one another. How miraculous are the transformations in our lives that come with even a small amount of spiritual practice. What a blessing it is to witness the activity of divine grace within, around, and among us. Let the divine purpose of spiritual awakening be foremost in your heart and mind as you embark on this program.

Start your group by asking the Divine to bring forth the spiritual friends who are exactly right for this experience. You may find the following suggestions helpful to forming and sustaining the group.

The Intention of Your Group

Begin by inviting those to join the group who share your interest in the principles and practices of the Eternal Way. The group intention to have clear spiritual focus will intensify the potential for individual growth and awakening. It may seem obvious that if people want to join a spiritual study group it is all for the same purpose. However, this is often not the case. People join groups for many different reasons—some to give and receive support with a particular endeavor such as practicing the Eternal Way, others for primarily social reasons, others for an opportunity to teach. Therefore the first important step in forming your group is clarity of purpose.

Clarity of purpose is essential.

When clarity of purpose for the prospective group members has been established, the next step is agreeing how you will operate as a group for the highest benefit of all. A basic plan for the term, meeting structure, and commitments of the members helps pave the way for a harmonious group experience. Over the years, students of this program have found the following guidelines helpful:

Establish guidelines for the group.

1. Those who join the group commit to participating fully in all group meetings by preparing homework material, attending every session on time, sharing in discussions, and following the group agreements.

2. Three agreements that have proven to support participation in the group are:

   • Members agree to maintain confidentiality of all group discussions. This helps create an atmosphere of safety and encourages individuals to speak truthfully about their experiences on the path.

   • Members agree to be mindful of the amount of time they spend talking in the group so that ample time exists for all members to participate.

- Members agree to listen to one another without judging or giving advice. This agreement is fundamental to the success of the group. Behind the agreement to refrain from offering advice or trying to enlighten others is faith. Faith is the recognition of Spirit indwelling each and every group member. Each member is respected as a spiritual being with their own direct connection to the Source. Members may choose, at any time, to ask for feedback from group members. This would then open the door to offering your perspective to another.

3. A weekly meeting is suggested to maintain the energetic contact with the individuals and the group process. Groups who attempt to meet less frequently tend to spend more time and energy reconnecting with group members and reestablishing the purpose and flow of the group.

4. Set and keep a spiritual context to the group through participation in group prayer and meditation.

5. An environment conducive to spiritual practice should be created for the meeting time. Select a meeting room that is quiet, comfortable, and without distractions or interruptions. Your spiritual focus can be enhanced by creating a simple altar for the group meetings, by burning a candle or incense.

Keep a spiritual context.

A Sample Course Outline

The subject matter of the course suggested below is readily applicable to a twelve week study group, or if a longer term is desired, twenty four weeks, spending two instead of one week on each topic.

Week One: Introduction to the group, the group structure, and intention

Introduction to the Eternal Way and the Fourfold Practice

Week Two: Contemplation: The Nature of
                Reality—Body, Mind, and Spirit

Week Three: Contemplation: The World Process

Week Four: The Practice of Meditation and
                Prayer

Week Five: Cultivating the Virtues:
                Harmlessness

Week Six: Cultivating the Virtues: Truthfulness

Week Seven: Cultivating the Virtues: Non-Stealing

Week Eight: Cultivating the Virtues: Right Use of
                Vital Force

Week Nine: Cultivating the Virtues:
                Non-Attachment

Week Ten: Cultivating the Virtues: Cleanliness

Week Eleven: Cultivating the Virtues:
                Contentment

Week Twelve: Surrender of the Sense of
                Separateness

                Group Closure

A Sample Meeting Outline

A two hour meeting each week is suggested to allow time for group meditation and discussion. It is important to begin and end your meeting on time. A sample evening meeting is outlined as follows:

7:00   Welcome of group members

	Brief review of the agenda for the meeting
	Opening prayer and meditation (approximately 20 minutes)
7:30	Facilitator introduces study topic
7:45	Group questions and discussion on the topic introduced
8:00	Group sharing on exercises done and practices experienced during the past week (the homework). This may be done in dyads, groups of four or six, or the entire group, depending on the size of your group
8:30	Facilitator briefly introduces topic for next week, reviews homework assignment and makes closing comments.
8:50	Closing Prayer and Meditation.

As the group progresses and the individuals become more proficient, it is appropriate to spend more time in silent meditation. A group new to meditation can start with ten minutes of prayer and silent meditation and progress to thirty minutes of silence.

Role of Facilitator

It is helpful to have a facilitator for the group. This may be an individual whose commitment it is to lead the group on a regular basis, or the facilitator's role may be shared equally by all group members through rotation. Shared facilitation leads to stronger involvement of the group as a whole, with each taking turns to prepare the introductory materials. The facilitator should plan ahead for introducing the new topic through study and review of the material. The facilitator for the meeting can also keep track of the meeting time schedule and support keeping the group on the point of focus.

Role of Prayer

Prayer opens the door of the mind to possibility.

As the group begins to open up and grow spiritually together, members may be inclined to support one another in current life challenges through prayer, a useful and spiritually sound contribution to one another's journey of awakening. It is essential that the spiritual practices the Eternal Way group is working on are relevant to the individual and their daily life circumstances. The "stuff" of our daily life is where we have the opportunity to test the spiritual principles, to become even-minded, and experience the power of faith.

While it is important in meetings to relate the challenges in one's daily life, it is equally important to find balance in that expression and to be able to open up to a new, more spiritually conscious perspective than is possible by just talking about it. Prayer can accomplish this.

One group invited members to come each week with an item for the group altar representing a particular inspiration or support to them on their journey. This item would be placed on the altar at the opening of the group, with a prayer.

A Conscious Conclusion

End each weekly group meeting with a short meditation and prayer of gratitude for the time spent together in God. Practice the discipline of keeping the spiritual focus of the group as members depart.

At the final meeting of the group, allow time for each participant to share the blessings they have received through the group and the spiritual awakening they have experienced. Some groups plan a simple prayer ritual to bring spiritual depth and meaning to the closure of the group and to signify their return to daily life with a new consciousness, a new way of being.

At the ritual closing of the group, participants can make a simple vow to practice the principles.

THE DEVOTEE'S VOW

I dedicate myself this day to spiritual growth
and awakening through studying the nature
of consciousness, cultivating the virtues,
practicing prayer and meditation, and
surrendering the sense of separateness.

I vow to practice harmlessness, truthfulness,
non-stealing, right use of vital force,
non-attachment, cleanliness, and contentment.

These vows I offer with a surrendered heart
in partnership with the Divine. May the lamp
of Truth always light my way.

Om   Peace   Amen

PRAYER FOR LIVING THE ETERNAL WAY

Open the eye of divine remembrance within me that I may see Your shining essence deep within the heart of all people. Open the eye of divine remembrance within me that I may see Your perfect plan in every situation. Help me let go of what I want, that I may receive the vision of truth You have prepared for me.

I have been blinded by sense attachments, by ignorance and fear. I am willing now to cast aside these false friends, to let go of that which no longer serves Your purpose. Grant me the courage to see clearly, without projection and without denial, Your sacred purpose for my life. May Your divine love strengthen me in the fulfillment of Your sacred purpose. May I never turn aside from the path of truth or refuse the light of Your love.

To be all that Your love calls me to be, to be an instrument of Your high purpose, to reveal the light of Your presence on earth, to be awake to Your presence, to see clearly the path You have set for me and to follow it without holding back, to sing forth Your praise, to rise in the morning with the joy of a willing heart, to rest in the evening with the peace of a soul who has seen, and followed, and lived according to Your way.

This is my prayer.

Om, Shanti, Peace, Amen.

RECOMMENDED READING

Aranya, Swami Hariharananda. *Yoga Philosophy of Patanjali.* Translation by P.N. Mukerji. Albany: State University of New York Press, 1983.

Byrom, Thomas (tr.) *The Dhammapada: The Sayings of the Buddha.* New York: Vintage Books, 1976.

Dass, Baba Hari. *Fire Without Fuel: The Aphorisms of Baba Hari Dass.* Edited by Ma Renu and Anand Dass Tabachnick, P.O. Box 2550, Santa Cruz, CA 95063: Sri Rama Publishing, 1986.

———. *Ashtanga Yoga Primer.* Edited by Ma Renu and Anand Dass Tabachnick, P.O. Box 2550, Santa Cruz, CA 95063: Sri Rama Publishing, 1981.

Davis, Roy Eugene. *An Easy Guide to Meditation.* P.O. Box 7, Lakemont, GA 30552: CSA Press, 1988.

———. *Light on the Spiritual Path.* P.O. Box 7, Lakemont, GA 30552: CSA Press, 1984.

———. *The Science of Kriya Yoga* P.O. Box 7, Lakemont, GA 30552: CSA Press, 1984.

———. *Life Surrendered in God: The Kriya Yoga Way of Soul Liberation.* P.O. Box 7, Lakemont, GA 30552: CSA Press, 1995.

de Mello, Anthony *The Song of the Bird.* New York: Image Books, 1984.

Drucker, Al. Sai Baba Gita: *The Way to Self-Realization and Liberation in This Age.* P.O. Box 337, Crestone, CO 81131: Atma Press, 1993.

Eliade, Mircea. *Yoga: Immortality and Freedom.* Translated by Willard R. Trask. Princeton, NJ: Princeton University Press, 1973.

Feuerstein, Georg. *Sacred Paths: Essays on Wisdom, Love, and Mystical Realization.* Larson Publications for the Paul Brunton Philosophical Foundation, 1991.

———. *The Yoga Sutra of Patanjali: A New Translation and Commentary.* Rochester, VT: Inner Traditions International, 1989.

———. *Yoga: the Technology of Ecstasy.* Los Angeles: Jeremy P. Tarcher, Inc., 1989.

Frawley, David. *From the River of Heaven: Hindu and Vedic Knowledge for the Modern Age.* P.O. Box 21713, Salt Lake City, Utah 84121: Passage Press, 1990.

Hixon, Lex. *Great Swan: Meetings with Ramakrishna.* Boston: Shambhala Publications, 1992.

Huxley, Aldous. *The Perennial Philosophy.* New York: Harper Colophon Books, 1945.

International Religious Foundation. *World Scripture: A Comparative Anthology of Sacred Texts.* New York: Paragon House, 1991.

Mitchell, Stephen (tr.) *Tao Te Ching.* New York: Harper and Row, 1988.

Miller, Barbara Stoler. *Yoga: Discipline of Freedom.* Berkeley, CA: University of California Press, 1996.

Natarajan, A. R. (ed.) *Sayings of Sri Ramana Maharshi.* Bangalore: Ramana Maharshi Center for Learning, 1996.

Nikhilananda, Swami. *Self-Knowledge: An English Translation of Sankaracharya's Atmabodha with Notes, Comments, and Introduction.* New York: Ramakrishna-Vivekananda Center, 1974.

Prabhavananda, Swami; Christopher Isherwood. *Bhagavad Gita: The Song of God.* Hollywood, CA: Vedanta Press, 1987.

Radhakrishnan, S. *The Bhagavad Gita with Introductory Essay, Sanskrit Text, English Translation and Notes.* 7/16 Ansari Road, New Delhi, India 110 002: Indus, 1993.

Raheem, Aminah. *Soul Return: Integrating Body, Psyche and Spirit.* 2621 Willowbrook Lane #104, Aptos, CA 95003: Process Accupressure, 1991.

Simon, Sidney B.; Leland W. Howe, Howard Kirschenbaum. *Values Clarification: A Handbook of Practical Strategies for Teachers and Students.* New York: Hart Publishing Company, Inc., 1972.

Vivekananda, Swami. *Karma Yoga and Bhakti Yoga.* New York: Ramakrishna-Vivekananda Center, 1982.

———. *Jnana Yoga.* New York: Ramakrishna-Vivekananda Center, 1982.

———. *Raja Yoga.* New York: Ramakrishna-Vivekananda Center, 1982.

Yogananda, Paramahansa. *The Autobiography of a Yogi.* Los Angeles: Self-Realization Fellowship, 1946.

GLOSSARY

Ahimsa
Virtue of Harmlessness. To refrain from harmful thoughts, words, and actions toward others and oneself. A yama of Eight-Limbed Yoga.

Ananda
Sanskrit word representing the quality of creative energy or bliss of the Godhead.

Aparigraha
Virtue of Non-Attachment or greedlessness. To rely solely on the true Self without attachment to possessions, people, or outcomes. A yama of Eight-Limbed Yoga.

Ashtanga Yoga
See Eight-Limbed Yoga

Asteya
Virtue of Non-Stealing. To be free of desire and covetousness. A yama of Eight-Limbed Yoga.

Aum
See Om.

Bhagavad Gita
A scripture of Hinduism translated as "The Song of God," in which dialog between Krishna and Arjuna reveals the divine guidance of Spirit to the seeking soul.

Bhakti Yoga
Yoga of love and devotion to the divine Presence.

Brahmacarya
Virtue of Right Use of Vital Force. To use one's energies to live in harmony with the divine purpose for one's life. A yama of Eight-Limbed Yoga.

Buddhi
Awakened intellect, the faculty of discernment.

Chit
Sanskrit word representing the quality of omniscience (consciousness) of the Godhead.

Classical Yoga
See Raja Yoga

Concentration Meditation
Meditation where the attention is directed to a single focus such as a mantra, the breath, or an image.

Dhammapada
A scripture of Buddhism which is a compilation of the teachings of the Buddha.

Fourfold Practice
The four main components of Kriya Yoga practice: study of the nature of consciousness, meditation, self-discipline, and surrender of sense of separateness.

Eight-Limbed Yoga
See Raja Yoga.

Eternal Way
The spiritual teaching with origins in the Vedas and the mystical lore of all world religions, also known as the Sanatana Dharma or the Perennial Philosophy.

Godhead
The initial manifestation of Supreme Consciousness (Spirit) as it moves from the transcendental realm toward creation of the world.

Hatha Yoga
Yoga of technique for balancing body/mind/spirit.

Jnana Yoga
Yoga of wisdom or discernment. Study, meditation, and inquiry lead to the experience of Pure Consciousness.

Karma Yoga
Yoga of selfless service. All work is done as worship of the Divine.

Koran
Sacred scripture of Islam.

Kriya Yoga
Yoga of purification through surrender, study, meditation, and self-discipline.

Kundalini Yoga
Yoga of technique for awakening the vital force of Spirit within the body/mind.

Laya Yoga
Yoga of technique for realization through contemplation of Om. Also known as Nada Yoga.

Maya
The fabric of nature from which the worlds are formed. This fabric is composed of atoms, space, time, and creative energy. Illusion which masks or covers the truth of the reality of Spirit.

Mindfulness Meditation
Meditation that emphasizes detached observation from one moment to the next of what arises in the body/mind.

Nada Brahma
The universal sound current, consisting of the reverberation set up between the outflow and reflux of creative energy, the Aum.

Niyama
Component of Eight-Limbed Yoga concerned with practice of the observances: cleanliness, contentment, self-discipline, study of the nature of consciousness, and surrender of the sense of separateness.

Om
The Sacred Word. The subtle energy of creation that arises between the outflowing force of divine creative energy and the returning force of awakened consciousness. The manifesting symbol of God. Known variously as Om, Amen, Aum, or Pranava. See Nada Brahma.

Patanjali
Author of the *Yoga Sutra*, a compilation of vedic wisdom delineating the practices of Kriya Yoga. Some historical estimates place him in the second century CE.

Prana
Vital force; life force.

Pranava
See Om.

Pranayama
Control or regulation of life force. A component of Eight-Limbed Yoga.

Raja Yoga
"Royal way" integrating study, meditation, surrendered devotion, and the practice of self-discipline. Also known as Ashtanga Yoga, Kriya Yoga, Classical Yoga, Eight-Limbed Yoga.

Rajas Guna
Neutralizing or active tendency in nature. The rajasic tendency causes restlessness and seeking sense-gratification.

Samadhi
Experience of Oneness with Spirit, the true Self. A component of Eight-Limbed Yoga.

Samtosha
Virtue of Contentment. To experience joy by dwelling continually in the remembrance of the true Self. A niyama of Eight-Limbed Yoga.

Sat
Sanskrit word representing the quality of omnipresence (being or existence) of the Godhead.

Sattva Guna
Positive, or uplifting tendency in nature. The sattvic tendency is elevating and causes health and spiritual awakening.

Satya
Virtue of Truthfulness. To bring thought, word, and action into harmony with one's divine nature. A yama of Eight-Limbed Yoga.

Shauca
Virtue of Cleanliness. To remove toxins from the body and mind so the true purity of the Self is perceived. A niyama of Eight-Limbed Yoga.

Superconscious Meditation
True meditation where awareness is resting in the Self, beyond the fluctuations of the mind.

Tamas Guna
Negative or downflowing tendency in nature. The tamasic tendency toward inertia leads to confusion and despair.

Tao
Chinese word translated as "the way" or "the path," considered to have three meanings: the way of ultimate reality, the way of the universe, and the way of human life.

Tao Te Ching
The basic scripture of Taoism. Translated as "The Book of the Way," a manual on the art of living in the Tao written by Lao-tzu in 5th century BCE.

Torah
Scripture containing the laws, teachings, and divine wisdom of Judaism. A compilation of revealed truth and ancient sacred commentaries.

Upanishads
The core scriptures of Hinduism. Sacred Vedic texts. See "Vedas."

Vedas
Ancient sacred writings of Hinduism and the source of yoga philosophy. The word "Veda" means "revealed truth" or knowledge.

Yamas
Component of Eight-Limbed Yoga concerned with practice of the restraints: harmlessness, truthfulness, non-stealing, right use of vital force, and non-attachment.

Yoga
To "yoke" or "bind back." A method of training designed to lead to integration or union with God. Known also as the science of Self-realization.

Yoga Sutra
Compilation of vedic wisdom by Patanjali. The aphorisms of the basic principles and practices of Kriya Yoga.

INDEX

For information about additional study aids available for your Eternal Way practice, to order additional copies of this book, to obtain information about the teaching schedule of the author, or to receive a schedule of spiritual programs and retreats, contact:

Center for Spiritual Enlightenment
1146 University Avenue
San Jose, California 95126

voice (408) 283-0221
www.CSEcenter.org
CSE@best.com